THE DOWNHOME SOUND

THE DOWNHOME SOUND

DIVERSITY and POLITICS in AMERICANA MUSIC

MANDI BATES BAILEY

Foreword by Guy Davis

LOUISIANA STATE UNIVERSITY PRESS
BATON ROUGE

Published by Louisiana State University Press
lsupress.org

Manufactured in the United States of America
First printing

Designer: Michelle A. Neustrom
Typeface: Sentinel
Printer and binder: Sheridan Books, Inc.

Charts 1.1, 1.2, 1.3, 4.1, 5.1, 5.2, and graphs 1.1 and 5.2 created by Mary Lee Eggart.

Cover images courtesy Maite Tiscar and Dan Cristian Pădure on Unsplash.

Library of Congress Cataloging-in-Publication Data

Names: Bailey, Mandi Bates, author. | Davis, Guy, 1952– writer of foreword.
Title: The downhome sound : diversity and politics in Americana music / Mandi Bates Bailey ; foreword by Guy Davis.
Description: Baton Rouge : Louisiana State University Press, 2023. | Includes bibliographical references and index.
Identifiers: LCCN 2022042847 (print) | LCCN 2022042848 (ebook) | ISBN 978-0-8071-7960-4 (paperback) | ISBN 978-0-8071-7916-1 (cloth) | ISBN 978-0-8071-7970-3 (pdf) | ISBN 978-0-8071-7969-7 (epub)
Subjects: LCSH: Americana (Music)—History and criticism. | Americana (Music)—Political aspects—United States.
Classification: LCC ML3512 .B35 2023 (print) | LCC ML3512 (ebook) | DDC 781.640973—dc23/eng/20220906
LC record available at https://lccn.loc.gov/2022042847
LC ebook record available at https://lccn.loc.gov/2022042848

for Ray Bates, Cecil Martin, and Jean Martin,

from a child thief

CONTENTS

FOREWORD

Americana has a lot of moving parts. Focusing on the sound of the music in isolation obscures the importance of the storytelling and the environment. That approach also relegates the music to passive description about historical moments. The music becomes a soundtrack rather than a tool. Understanding culture is vital to understanding those of us who see ourselves as, at least partially, in the Pete Seeger tradition. For us, we are teachers and artists that use the music to impact as well as inform.

President Barack Obama underscored not only Seeger but the social value in American roots music in a statement following the singer's 2014 death. "Once called 'America's tuning fork,' Pete Seeger believed deeply in the power of song," he professed. "But more importantly, he believed in the power of community—to stand up for what's right, speak out against what's wrong, and move this country closer to the America he knew we could be. Over the years, Pete used his voice—and hammer—to strike blows for workers' rights and civil rights; world peace and environmental conservation. And he always invited us to sing along. For reminding us where we come from and where we need to go, we will always be grateful to Pete Seeger."[1] This statement reflects the role of community and the power of the music to do more than describe.

I call myself an American Roots musician. I'm in folk, I'm in the blues, I have a one-man play, but they're all part of each other.[2] Americana just works that way. It's a culture that embraces different musical styles, attracts diverse people, and conveys a message—either directly through lyrics or implicitly by reflecting the environment it binds together. This book assesses Americana in that vein. It considers the message, those of us who write/sing those messages, the audience that seeks them out, and the ultimate effect on people who don't identify with the Americana culture at all.

Reaching beyond the community to grow and educate is pivotal, but this research tells us that potential is great but growth is hard and brings additional challenges. That message sounds like a lot of what we do in this culture—we can't be afraid to talk or sing about our own struggles. That's a key to what we do. It keeps us authentic and allows our message to resonate. If wide exposure dulls that impact, do we even want it? How can we not if the exposure could inform and open hearts and minds?

The question and answer are circular. Well-written songs often carry that burden—to entertain while encouraging deeper contemplation. The nature of artists like me is to expand beyond a narrowly defined musical or even broad artistic space much like the nature of music in this culture is to transcend boundaries. To that end, we don't provide the answers as much as we create a space for others to question the world, the country, and even themselves.

This book describes the artists, the music, the community, and teaches us that Americana is more than a soundtrack, but mostly it generates important questions that aren't easy to answer.

—Guy Davis

PREFACE

Certainties relating to Wikipedia—it's flawed (see Rector 2008), and it's pervasive (see Vetter 2018). Indeed, most objects, prominent people, and places have a Wikipedia page. Round Pond, Maine, does not. Try looking for Round Pond in Wikipedia; you'll be directed to nearby Bristol.

Jenny Cleaves describes Round Pond as a "darling little fishing village" (pers. interview, July 5, 2021). Appreciation for rural Maine and her children leaked into every aspect of our morning conversation. Two things were certain following that dialogue—I wanted to see Slaid, Jenny's son, and Rod Picott perform together live, and I wanted to visit Round Pond before the circus arrives. "It's ridiculous," Jenny says of the multimillion-dollar homes being constructed near quaint New England cottages (pers. interview, July 5, 2021).

Slaid Cleaves wasn't born in Round Pond or in South Berwick, Maine, where he was raised, however. Cleaves was born in Washington, DC, in 1964 while his father was a graduate student in psychology at George Washington University. The 1960s were a tumultuous decade generally, but DC saw protests, its residents were finally given the right to vote for president with the ratification of the twenty-third amendment, and the Civil Rights Act of 1964 was passed. Slaid's parents wanted to raise him and the three children that followed in a less turbulent environment. The resultant move to a South Berwick farm provided a more provincial setting where the Cleaves children could learn about life as well as human behavior. Jenny is quick to note of her then husband, Craig, "there were no psychologists up here in the seventies. He worked in clinics, and Slaid learned about life at the table" (pers. interview, July 5, 2021).

According to Jenny, her son was always introspective and writing. In the second grade, Slaid's interest in music joined his interest in writing when she took him to a sale held at a South Berwick convent, where she bought an upright piano for twenty-five dollars.

Not long after his mother purchased the piano, Slaid met a kindred spirit in Rod Picott. A year younger than Slaid, Rod jokes that they identified as writers even then. Slaid even recalls a conversation riding the school bus home about wanting to be artists when they grew up. He says fans get a kick out of their history. Seeing why is as easy as seeing their link to what would become the Americana format—both appreciate acoustic music and songwriting, and I've lost count of the Tom Petty and Bruce Springsteen references in our conversations.

Upon discovering an error in one of my early drafts of this book in which I referred to Rod as "Roderick," Slaid emailed, writing, "only my mom (and the IRS, I suppose) calls Rod 'Roderick'" (pers. interview, March 24, 2021). Slaid's teasing smirk came through, and I knew I had to talk to Jenny.

Slaid and Rod maintained their songwriting dream throughout childhood. Slaid recalls grudgingly accepting piano lessons when he wanted to learn guitar. He performed Beethoven for his year-end recital when he was fifteen. He performed Springsteen's "Jungleland," complete with saxophone accompaniment, the following year for his final recital. Jenny recounts the performance with great pride. She later learned Springsteen served as a catalyst for Slaid to pick up the guitar. "Demonstrates how powerful a stripped-down acoustic album can be," Slaid says of Springsteen's *Nebraska* (pers. interview, February 24, 2021).

Jenny and Rod, whom she indeed consistently refers to as Roderick, recall a more difficult early educational path for Rod. He saw the Cleaves home as a refuge from the turmoil of his own. He addresses his adolescent angst and brooding behavior in ways that leave one thinking a song he cowrote with Slaid, "Black T-Shirt" (2009), is at least semiautobiographical. Nevertheless, despite the darkness that is a frequent undercurrent in his music, I have difficulty seeing the smiling affable man that frequently laughed and ran his fingers through his hair during our first meeting as perpetually brooding. Perhaps this is a lesson from both Slaid and Rod's songwriting—pushing forward yet rooted in experience. Jenny used the word "hopeful" to describe the way her son and his friend address struggle, strife, and emo-

Rod (*left*) and Slaid, circa 1980.

tional challenges in their writing (pers. interview, July 5, 2021). My characterization was "dignified." Hers is better.

"He was always very tall and very intellectual," Jenny says of Rod. She worked as a tutor in the elementary school he and Slaid attended, recommending Rod, then a year behind his friend, be advanced a grade (pers. interview, July 5, 2021). His high school administrators finally agreed, and the pair graduated at the same time. Could there really have been another outcome?

Slaid and Rod have different approaches but reach the same conclusion when describing their first public performance. Logistical details play large in Slaid's description. Emotion colors Rod's. The former involves planning, band names, and choice of music. I get the sense that Slaid approaches writing and performing as if taking disparate pieces from a variety of puzzles and creating something intriguingly new. My impression of Rod is that feelings wash over him and he rolls with them. "It was a complete disaster . . . At the end of three songs we were completely demoralized," Rod says of the first time he and Slaid played publicly together at a high school assembly (pers. interview, April 12, 2021). He ripped all the strings from his guitar afterward.

Emotion and problem-solving have played into their approaches to building careers as well. Slaid, and his wife, Karen, searched for music towns after he finished college in Boston. Desiring to further his career away from the Boston expense, traffic, and weather—and inspired by the 1991 *Rolling Stone* headline "Heaven with a Texas Zip Code"—the couple road-tripped to the Lone Star State. According to Slaid, "Seattle was too wet. Minneapolis was too cold. Athens seemed to be fading, but Austin . . ." (pers. interview, February 24, 2021).

Rod, on the other hand, landed in Boulder, Colorado, and later moved to Nashville, where he felt his star rise. "Somehow I'd gotten it in my head that I could move to Nashville and become a staff writer at one of the big publishing companies. This is sort of funny because looking back there was nothing indicating that this was at all possible" (pers. interview, April 12, 2021). Nevertheless, he arrived in Tennessee and resolved to improve his writing, looking to the likes of giants such as Lucinda Williams, John Prine, and Guy Clark.

Slaid admits to being insular and protective of his work initially. But he could trust Rod. "I knew that he was not going to bring something out of left field to the table that I'd have to politely decline. And, even more importantly, I knew that he could be honest with me and point out, with a thoughtful argument, why an idea of mine was not up to snuff" (pers. interview, February 24, 2021).

With fifty years of friendship behind them and more than eight hundred miles between them, Slaid and Rod still write together and trust still characterizes their process. "We know each other so well that we don't have to dance around a song we're working on. We are very blunt . . . I remember a writing session at his home when he first moved to Austin and Slaid's wife thought we were fighting. We were simply writing," Rod says, before becoming deferential to Slaid. "He's very skilled where I'm weak and I'm quite good at his weakness . . . if he has one" (pers. interview, April 12, 2021).

A nearly lifelong regard and mutual admiration has colored my communication with the two men. Slaid has said on multiple occasions that Rod doesn't get the credit he deserves, while Rod frequently addresses the beauty in Slaid's voice. They seem to straddle the fence between little boys vociferously defending teammates and grown men recognizing that one's heroes are closer than realized. Notably, Slaid read a poem written by Rod at his own father's funeral.

Hippies or cowboys? I don't know either fits those molds, but one can't miss the Guthrie in Slaid or the roughness in Rod's voice. It's fitting that these two men, who recognized their respective roles in what would become Americana before the format existed, are based in Texas and Tennessee. It's also fitting that their roots are elsewhere. After all, Americana's roots are difficult to trace.

ACKNOWLEDGMENTS

This book is the result of contributions by artists and others in this musical space, colleagues, friends, and family.

I am thankful to those who have provided guidance throughout my career. Drs. Mark Peffley (University of Kentucky) and Rich Fording (University of Alabama) have supported me for much longer than mentors expect. Likewise, I'm sure Dr. Jeffrey Fine (Clemson University) expected to be rid of me following graduate school, but he has been a consistent voice of reason for two decades. I likewise value and need Dr. Steven Nawara's (Lewis University) voice. Undoubtedly, anything I produce involves discussion with Mark, Rich, Jeff, and Steve. I'm blessed they tolerate me.

Drs. Horace Bartilow (American University), Michael Baun (Valdosta State University), and James Druckman (Northwestern University) have similarly become dear friends and valuable critical eyes. I'm grateful for their guidance and affirmation.

I thank Drs. Lakeyta Bonnette-Bailey (Georgia State University), Tiffany Willoughby-Herard (University of California, Irvine), Carol Glen (Valdosta State University), James LaPlant (Valdosta State University), Robert Harding (Valdosta State University), Yu Ouyang (Purdue University Northwest), Zachary Karazsia (Valdosta State University), Joseph Robbins (Valdosta State University), Bernard Tamas (Valdosta State University), Anthony "Jack" Gierzynski (University of Vermont), Jody Baumgartner (East Carolina University), Daniel Baraskay (Valdosta State University), Mary-Kate Lizotte (Augusta University), Paul Vincent (Valdosta State University), Cigdem Sirin (University of Texas at El Paso), and Lucas Church. Without Lakeyta's book and a comment by Joe, this book would not exist. Tiffany and

Zack's unwavering support, Yu, Dan, and Mary-Kate's willingness to administer the survey, Carol, James, Robert, Yu, Jody, Joe, and Bernie's willingness to talk about the project when they likely didn't find it nearly as interesting as I did, Jack's suggestions and theoretical contributions, Paul's map design, and Cigdem's personal observations were all invaluable. Similarly, I can't thank Lucas enough for his encouragement to utilize a personal frame. I was reticent about the approach, but he knew better.

There are a number of people in this musical space who don't get much public praise yet work tirelessly. I've been fortunate to meet several of them. Jon Bernstein, Sarah Bennett, Karen Cleaves, Lisa Jenkins, Maggie Mitchell, Erin Scholze, Kristin Starling, Ken Weinstein, Thom Wolke, and Lee Zimmerman deserve thanks. Mary Muse and Aengus Finnan gave substantial time for this out-of-the-box project. Their insights enabled me to reimagine the introduction and better understand the culture, and Aengus even offered financial support. Chad Staehly, thank you for your efforts, advice, and encouragement. Photographers Russell Cusick, Neale Eckstein, Stacie Huckeba, James Martin, Seth Roffman, Stefan Sobell, Michelle Stancil, Jay Stausser, John Zara, and particularly Nick Barber contributed images that brought far more life to this book than tables, graphs, charts, and statistical models can provide. And thanks to senior editor Neal Novak at LSU Press, who shepherded this book through the publication process.

Nelson Gullett has been a friend since we were undergraduates at Morehead State University. I appreciate his insights, and I'm pleased this project enabled us to reconnect. I have been similarly pleased to meet Jenny Cleaves and became closer with Cigdem Sirin and José Villalobos (both of the University of Texas at El Paso) through this process.

The artists contributing to this book gave their time, well-reasoned and at times potentially uncomfortable assessments, and in some cases unreleased work. They are extraordinarily talented, socially aware, brilliant, and—most important—*kind.* I could write pages of thanks to each of them. In the spirit of brevity, I hope that my writing signals both the value of their input and the depth of my appreciation. I'm regularly asked, "How'd you get these people to talk to you?" My response, "I asked."

Several artists did more than agree to interviews, they facilitated greater learning and made themselves continually available. Slaid Cleaves, Robbie Fulks, Irakli Gabriel, Colin Gilmore, Will Kimbrough, Jesse Langlais,

Tim O'Brien, Darrell Scott, and John Paul White absolutely went above and beyond. I am humbled by their kindness and generosity. Admittedly, I felt badass for the first times in my life when I received text messages (in separate conversations) from Tim O'Brien and Darrell Scott, and I immediately called my dad. Prior to publication of this book, I did not mention that to them. I'm no longer stunned when I hear from them, I'm excited to learn more.

When I began this project, I was apprehensive about the qualitative portions of the research. Truthfully, I just wanted to get through the interviews with as little embarrassment as possible to get to what is more comfortable. While I was not surprised by the caliber of conversation, given the quality of the songwriting, I was surprised by some of the personal connections made. I welcome every opportunity to engage BettySoo, Eliza Gilkyson, and Bernice Lewis. Finally, to Rod Picott and Reggie Harris, you're beautiful men. Thank you is insufficient.

I find expressing the depth of my gratitude to Guy Davis similarly difficult. While finding time to participate in an interview can be difficult, the time necessary to review manuscript materials and contribute a foreword required a considerable investment in time and energy. Guy completed the forward amid staging a one-man show.

I turn now to the young people that made notable contributions. To my niece, Wynter Bailey, Mary Alex Carter, and Kiana Johnson, I appreciate your assistance in the identification of popular music. I blame focus on my family for my lack of awareness of popular culture, but in reality I'm hopeless and impatient. I suspect my inadequacies were amusing, but you're far too polite to say as much.

I thank Scarlett Bailey, Stephanie Brown, Shannon Johnson, Rebecca Craft-Carlos, Lois Edwards, Sid Bundy, and Katie Triechel, women for whom sister is not quite sufficient but nevertheless appropriate. I'm similarly grateful to my parents, Jeff and Lynn Bates. Finally, my "band" deserves a more full-throated thank you than I can possibly muster. My husband, Kerry, and our children, Irie-Jean, Oliver, and Gus, encourage me in ways I don't always appreciate, but always need.

THE DOWNHOME SOUND

›››››››› INTRODUCTION ‹‹‹‹‹‹‹‹

THE DOWNHOME SOUND

They played dances, made the rounds. Galax to Rocky Mount. The tunes they knew no one could count. It was all in their heads and hands.

—Robbie Fulks, "Aunt Peg's New Old Man" (2016)

Valdosta State University, like colleges and universities across the United States, dismissed students from physical classes in March 2020 in the wake of the COVID-19 pandemic. Professors, administrators, staff, and students returned to an entirely different campus experience the following August. Stepping into the classroom was a regular reminder of the changing world around us—socially distanced desks meant most classes were divided such that students were at best attending classes once each week, masked faces filled the rooms, and there was no leaning in to provide an encouraging word. Amid this relative academic dystopia, my fall schedule included a great deal of time in my office between classes, but the typical chatter among colleagues and students had largely evaporated. Silence punctuated by the releasing cracks and thuds of opening and closing doors in our office suite filled the resulting void.

I can't work in silence. Music files and Pandora playlists provided two opportunities. First, they filled the silence, allowing me to focus on writing, grading, etc. Second, the music gave me an excuse to periodically walk into the common suite area and ask if the music was too loud or bothersome. The answer was never yes. During one of my more productive moments, Dr. Joseph Robbins approached my office as Jason Isbell sang and wondered aloud about the political leanings of Isbell's audience. As he spoke, I noticed

Dr. Lakeyta Bonnette-Bailey's book, *Pulse of the People: Political Rap Music and Black Politics,* on my desk. This is the point I fell into this research, but it isn't the beginning.

A decade before the pandemic I was invited to participate in a conference on post-racialism at the University of Nebraska—Lincoln. As an assistant professor, recently removed from my doctoral program and *very* aware of my southern Appalachian accent and the inability of my mouth to keep up with my mind, the conference was initially intimidating despite the efforts of the late Dr. Michael Combs, who was generous to include me. At the opening dinner I felt as if I was the only person there that didn't know everyone else. I took an open seat at a table that happened to be filled with only Nebraska professors. There were two empty seats to my left. Dr. Bonnette-Bailey sat next to me and began talking to me as if we had been raised together. We talked more about our daughters than our research that weekend, but I soon became familiar with her work. I initially thought meeting her was the beginning of this project. It wasn't.

I realized the origins of this research during a phone call with Darrell Scott, who was coincidentally visiting family near Lincoln, Nebraska. Mr. Scott and I chatted about Kentucky and the generational impact of music. I thought about a similar conversation with Rodney Crowell (who also has some Kentucky roots), and I realized in that moment that, aside from fondness for old hounds, good Bloody Marys, and badly burned toast, music is likely all my dad and I have in common. My mind drifted to attending a few shows with him and a moment during graduate school when he called to ask me to join him in east Tennessee to see Steve Earle. I had not told my parents that I had taken off to Boston that weekend.

My youngest son joined me during the interview with Mr. Scott, and the conversation turned to my children sharing their mother and grandfather's musical tastes. "See, your family is an example," Mr. Scott observed before our conversation turned to my being raised and educated in a regional "hotbed" of strong roots music (pers. interview, April 15, 2021).

Darrell Scott ignited my memory. I considered the obvious moments—my now-husband, Kerry, taking me to see Bob Dylan for my birthday after we began dating and then giving our daughter the middle name Dylan a few years later; Kerry withdrawing his phone from his pocket when we met Will Kimbrough and Will saying, "Prom Pic," before beaming; our searching Corpus Christi and Port Aransas for dive bars with good music during our time in Texas, which included traveling to San Antonio to see Todd Snider play with John Prine; Kerry arguing with me about my seeing Robert Earl Keen without him at the Birchmere in Alexandria; taking our children to see Old Crow Medicine Show in St. Augustine; the way our older son is instantly calmed when hearing Amanda Shires and Jason Isbell cover Warren Zevon's "Mutineer" (1995); laughing at our younger son, a toddler, when he sings Corb Lund's "The Gothest Girl I Can" (2012). Then I dug deeper. I recalled shows, particularly Tim O'Brien, Buddy Miller, and Robbie Fulks at the Laurel Theatre in Knoxville, The Dame in Lexington, and Southgate House in Newport, Kentucky, respectively.

I remembered a sorority sister, Jessica Harwood, introducing me to Todd Snider in college. A few years later I visited her in Atlanta, and we went to a show. It wasn't Snider, but after we returned to her apartment she gave me *Songs for the Daily Planet* on CD with a sideways glance and the corner of her lip drawn.[1] I remembered the first time I ever saw Dylan play in Knoxville, wondering if the venue would be filled with old people. I recalled driving to Cincinnati with Todd to see Steve Earle and witnessing the dichotomous reactions of the crowd when Earle sang "John Walker Blues" (2002). I remembered waking the morning after a friend's wedding wondering if she would continue to have time for me and subsequently driving from Louisville to Birmingham to attend a music festival.

I recalled one of the few times during college I woke on a Sunday morning resolved to attend church. A friend had recommended a church somewhere outside of Morehead. I got lost shortly after driving from the off-ramp. These were days when one didn't have the option of Google Maps readily available on their phone. I didn't find the church, but I found a bluegrass festival. John Paul White tells me that bluegrass is like religion, so I'm absolved of guilt. Later, I recalled another sorority sister, Sid, laughing about finding herself near Cave Run Lake in Kentucky at what appeared to be a dive bar listing to live bluegrass music. "Old man jam session" was her characterization.

I recalled meeting someone in Knoxville who, perhaps unbeknownst to him, gave me the tools to see the music I enjoyed as a collectivity and introduced me to new artists and impressive local music, which included RB Morris's beautiful cover of John Prine's "Late John Garfield Blues" (1972). Morris graced me with an interview for this book.

Most of my friends would say that I have a terrible memory, and they would be correct. I nevertheless reeled from the memories following my conversation with Mr. Scott. Suddenly I was a little girl on my grandparents' front porch in the head of the holler. I would never have admitted it until I was grown and long-since moved away, but I loved breaking beans with my grandmother. I loved staring down the hill at the dirt road where Stephanie and I rode ten-speed bikes toward the creek past the rusted-out pickup and derelict corn crib that had been converted to storage space. But mostly I loved the sounds. The paper bag that held unbroken beans would rustle as Mamaw folded the rim, creating a wide cuff at the top enabling her to see into the bag as she leaned over the arm of a gray, weathered rocking chair positioned to the side of the front door. She would withdraw a handful of beans and deposit them onto her lap before selecting a slim, green victim. She then snapped off an end in such a way that she instantaneously peeled back a fragile corkscrew, revealing a darker seam down the center of the bean. Then a firm resounding crack, crack, crack, crack. I was never able to produce the potent crack when breaking beans. I blame the beans. Mamaw then discarded the corkscrew into a growing lime green wig on the porch floor and placed the bean fragments into an enormous stainless steel bowl that had been dented so frequently that the dents appeared a purposeful aesthetic decision on the part of the manufacturer. Her long, thick fingernails scratched rhythmically against the metal. Meanwhile, Papaw sat in a twin rocker flanking the opposite side of the door smoking and quietly singing "Up on Cripple Creek."[2] I had no idea who The Band was at the time. Recalling my maternal grandfather easily transitioned to remembering my paternal grandfather and finally discovering the origin of this book.

My father's father lived "across the hill" from us. I could walk across a narrow trail that created a crease in the steep incline of the mountain that connected our house to his, often encountering murky pools filled with black tadpoles. During one visit, I decided to clean his truck. I'm not sure what possessed me. He would have never asked me to clean, and while my memory is lacking I don't recall being a kid that enjoyed anything resembling work. Nevertheless, I now remember very vividly cleaning the center console. A Styrofoam cup containing a paper towel soaked with saliva and what was once wintergreen Skoal was the centerpiece. I wish it had been Copenhagen. That would make for a better story. I was disgusted by the ghastly paper towel. Perhaps that's the reason I looked inside the glovebox—to see something less revolting. There I found three cassettes. Two were Jimmy Buffett. The other was Jerry Jeff Walker. I was intrigued, and I stole them. I'm sure he knew that I took them, but he never mentioned it. That's the origin—wintergreen Skoal, cassette tapes, and a child thief.

These memories illustrate not only my experiences with this music, but also slices of the culture that surround it. My memory is punctuated not just with guitars, harmonicas, mandolins, fiddles, and thoughtful rich lyrics, it's also colored by dirt roads, hollers, festivals, dive bars, amphitheaters, and interactions with other fans and staff as well as the artists. Indeed, when Rod Picott discusses Americana, the culture and venues are pivotal: "We all came up in the same bars. . . . It was this beautiful sort of gathering place. It was like someone opened a home where everybody was invited. You know?" (pers. interview, April 12, 2021).

The more I considered Picott's words, the more I realized that *I did know,* at least in part, but did everyone else? Much of this music lyrically reflects diversity as well as the inclusivity Picott describes, but that doesn't mean that American roots music intuitively signals that it is the home Picott found in the early days of Americana.[3] As a heterosexual white woman that teaches and studies minority politics, I'm often an outsider. Despite the warm welcome I have always received from colleagues, many of whom have become close personal friends, I'm always aware I'm a bit different. I wouldn't say feeling embraced yet somewhat outside is uncomfortable—I've never felt uncomfortable. But I am aware I'm different. I wonder if the broad Americana culture is seen in a similar way by minority fans.

There is certainly diversity in the origins of roots music, but that doesn't mean that minorities are represented across the industry. In fact, the artists interviewed in this volume want to increase their appeal to diverse audiences, they just aren't always quite sure how to do it. Further, appeal isn't limited to attending live shows. Much as Americans could benefit from learning about minority politics even if they don't consider themselves members of specific minority groups, African Americans, LGBTQ+ Americans, Latinx Americans, Asian Americans, Native Americans, etc., could appreciate and connect to Americana if they saw how the music reflects their experiences, and in turn incorporated the music into their lives.

After all, as Aengus Finnan, folk artist and executive director of Folk Alliance International, poignantly says, "people are listening in their backyards and on their front porches" (pers. interview, May 18, 2021).[4] To that end, cultural commonalities and distinctions in this musical space are considered below.

The Downhome Sound

Bob Dylan sang, "How many roads must a man walk down before you call him a man?"[5] Howlin' Wolf asked, "How many more years have I got to let you dog me around?"[6] John Prine crooned about the Indian Sabu's trek from "the jungles of East St. Paul."[7] Pete Seeger used his voice as a hammer to "ring in love between my brothers and sisters all over this land."[8] Jason Isbell took the stage at the Americana Music Awards in 2018 and belted out, "I'm a white man looking in a Black man's eyes wishing I'd never been one of the guys. We pretended not to hear another white man's joke. Oh, the times ain't forgotten."[9] American roots music, comprised of many constituent genres, has long been associated with politics, diversity, and race, but political science has yet to explore the impact of Americana music.

This research begins to fill that void by considering the message, the artists, the culture, and the impact. In turn, I use a mixed-methods approach consisting of lyrical analyses, interviews with Americana artists, interviews with music journalists and festival organizers, and a survey-based experiment to explain the intended messages, the audience reaction, and the consequences of exposure to unfamiliar listeners. Ultimately, personal interviews with artists point to the desire for inclusion, diversity, and, in some cases, the need to address racial and/or societal injustices directly. Analyses of the survey-based experiment reveal that exposure to Americana music is related to more positive assessments of African Americans, immigrants, and the LGBTQ+ community relative to commercial country music and rap music.

American roots music is difficult to define. Constituent genres include—but aren't limited to—folk, bluegrass, country, blues, southern rock, rock and roll, jazz, and cowpunk. Americana has become a blanket term to cover music that fits comfortably within these genres or incorporates elements from a combination of them. Lee David Zimmerman writes about the artists and music that share a unique culture and finds that the diversity in the music reflects the varied audiences that seek truth in music: "There's something for everyone" (pers. interview, February 11, 2021). This introduction walks readers through a brief history, focusing on the regional musical development across the heartland with an eye toward racial and socioeconomic diversity.

Artists Cody Canada, Slaid Cleaves, Irakli Gabriel, Colin Gilmore, Anana Kaye, Will Kimbrough, Bernice Lewis, RB Morris, and Joel Rafael all point to Americana as a label that aids in marketing (pers. interviews, February–December 2021). Rafael, a Californian, points to the origins of Americana music as a radio format in southern California (pers. interview, April 2, 2021). Indeed, fans of this music may be surprised to learn that a radio station located in suburban Los Angeles pioneered a format based on the amalgamation of American roots music that we now recognize as Americana. Thus, the radio format began in neither the southern United States nor a rural area.[10] Darrell Scott further underscores the fallacy of strictly southern origins by noting that he, and other Americana music pioneers, including those associated with Massachusetts-based Rounder Records, met in Squam Lake, New Hampshire, to discuss the promotion of the genre (pers. interview April 15, 2021).

This introductory chapter offers a brief exploration of the development of the constituent genres of Americana before presenting the plan of the book. Bluegrass, blues, country, cowpunk, folk, gospel, jazz, rock and roll, rockabilly, and southern rock all contribute to Americana music and can be seen in the activities of the Americana Music Association, a nonprofit organization dedicated to increasing awareness of the genre that was founded in 1999.[11] The roots of the constituent genres and the Americana Music Association establish both racial diversity and the need to look to stereotyping as a theoretical framework for understanding the impact of the music.

Nevertheless, keeping in mind that many artists, organizers, and fans of the constituent genres seek to maintain varying levels of purity in the music they play, support, and consume while others embrace a more eclectic musical approach is imperative. For example, BettySoo, Slaid Cleaves, Irakli Gabriel, Anana Kaye, Rod Picott, and Darrell Scott identify as Americana artists. Cleaves is quick to note that his work falls "closer to folk" if Americana music is assessed on a continuum, however (pers. interview, February 24, 2021).

Similarly, Kristen Englenz embraces the Americana label, noting that it fits her because Americana is "a descriptor for the genre-less" (pers. in-

Slaid Cleaves at Foxlowe Arts Center, Leek, UK, on September 28, 2017. Courtesy Nick Barber.

terview, July 26, 2021). Gabriel and Kaye, international artists, embrace a variety of roots music but note, "It's Americana in the nitty gritty" (pers. interview, February 13, 2021). Darrell Scott embraces the diversity in the Americana label, underscoring that the diversity in his work is characteristic of the diversity in the musical space (pers. interview, April 15, 2021). Alternatively, several artists, such as Todd Snider, associate primarily with folk music (pers. interview, May 21, 2021). Grammy-nominated artist Eliza Gilkyson also sees herself as a folk artist primarily, and she actively seeks to preserve the purity of folk music (pers. interview, April 8, 2021). Patterson Hood and Robbie Fulks similarly identify first with their preferred constituent genres. Hood emphatically states, "We're a rock and roll band" (pers.

interview, February 19, 2021). Likewise, Fulks embraces country while noting that stylistically that's where he is most comfortable (pers. interview, April 19, 2021). Meanwhile, John Paul White, who won two Grammys for Best Country Duo/Group Performance and one for Best Folk Album as one-half of The Civil Wars, rejects labeling entirely. When asked how he would label himself if forced, White responds, "I'm not sure I know yet. I'm not sure that I want to know" (pers. interview, May 10, 2021).

The chorus of "Welding Burns," a cowritten song by Slaid Cleaves and Rod Picott, begins "Some things you're born to, some things you gotta learn."[12] This lyric speaks to blue-collar labor, but it also speaks to specific cultural origins of Americana music and explains the necessity in understanding that the music reflects varied regions, racial and ethnic roots, and socioeconomic backgrounds. More specifically, Americana music, like many of the constituent genres that contribute to it, is informed by different cultures.

In the Beginning . . .

The origins of gospel music, even broadly conceived, are far more difficult to establish than pinpointing the beginning of the Americana radio format. Darden (2004, 7) states, "To understand American music, you must first understand the spirituals and gospel music." Indeed African roots may have supplied the drum beat, but the institution of slavery in the American South and the resultant need to purge the demons of slavery through spirituals that were not quite yet hymns or even written and always sung with lyrical precision led to development of American gospel music and distinct forms of American folk music (Darden 2004).

W. E. B. Du Bois (1903) illustrates a tie between gospel and American folk music in his seminal treatise, *The Souls of Black Folks:* "by fateful chance the Negro folk-song—the rhythmic cry of the slave—stands today not simply as the sole American music, but as the most beautiful expression of human experience born this side of the seas." Certainly, in the United States, race is often integral in determining who the "folk" are in folk music.[13] This focus on the people is the emphasis of folk music, which, like the Americana umbrella that guides this research, leaves folk music divided among constituent genres. For example, Folk Alliance International (FAI), a nonprofit organization dedicated to the preservation and promotion of folk music, specifically recognizes a variety of music types within folk, such as Appalachian, bluegrass, blues, and even Americana and hip-hop that may or may not be geographically aligned.[14]

Therefore, while this research looks to folk as a component of the Americana format which ties together seemingly disparate genres, a distillation of Americana music would fit within folk, which is connected to several of the constituent genres. This suggests that while the *Honky Tonk Amnesia* radio format pioneered in southern California was the first to promote American roots music as a collectivity, FAI took a similar approach with some of the Americana constituent genres just a few years later in 1989. Both *Honky Tonk Amnesia* and the establishment of FAI occurred before the foundation of the Americana Music Association.

Regardless of the type of American folk music, there is a decidedly leftist political flavor that often takes on nostalgic thematic elements related to the "common man" (Roy 2010). Undeniably, the "common man" is integral to both folk and Americana. It is the lifeblood of the music. Not all Americans recognize that the "common man" takes many forms, however.

The common man may be the Native American in New Mexico, as depicted in Pueblo music of indigenous North Americans, the poor, white, southern Appalachian coal miner depicted in bluegrass music with Irish origins, or the African American in the Mississippi Delta whose ancestors participated in the field hollers that would evolve into the blues. Perhaps legendary music archivist Alan Lomax (1947) illustrated the link between American roots music and international/indigenous origins best in his characterization of Negro prison songs: "These songs belong to the musical traditions which Africans brought to the New World, but they are also as American as the Mississippi River. They are born out of the very rock and earth of this country."[15]

Roy (2010) illustrates that the culture surrounding American roots music has always been more inclusive than the broader political/social climate may have been. Yet despite the deep complexity in racial/ethnic and cultural roots, the dominant image of the folk artist in some ways remains white, unkempt, and guitar-toting with a harmonica affixed to his neck, not unlike the images evoked of the 1960s folk revival, which featured, among others, Bob Dylan and Neil Young (Lornell 2012).

This image is occasionally supplanted by the cowboy hat-adorned outlaw, which strangely enough resulted from record label marketing in the 1970s. I say strangely because Americana artists and audiences typically look to the medium as an escape from widely disseminated popular music despite the superstardom several folk artists achieved during the 1960s folk revival and the fact that music often labeled as Americana may achieve more financial and critical success than other forms of roots music. Nevertheless, outlaw/progressive/alternative country arose with RCA's release of the compilation album *Wanted! The Outlaws* in 1976.[16] The album featured Jessie Colter, Tompall Glaser, Waylon Jennings, and Willie Nelson and was a commercial success in both country and popular music. In fact, *Wanted! The Outlaws* "became country music's first platinum album and introduced the outlaw label to the masses" (Streissguth 2013, 3). Ironically, it was commercial success that Fraser (2018) suggests was a catalyst for Jennings and Nelson renegotiating their contracts so that they had more creative control and the ability to reform their brand of country music to what resembles the outlaw country movement seen within Americana.

The disassociation with more commercial music is a prevalent theme throughout Americana. Town Mountain, for instance, addresses the concept lyrically in "Underdog": "No I never got much notice from that record company man. He listens to my music but he just don't understand. Looking down upon me from his hotel suite so high. Lord he wouldn't know a rounder if it looked him in the eye. Says he can't do nothing for me so I thank him for his time. It's a country music club, he's got me standing in line. But don't think for a moment you can put me on a shelf. I'll make the breaks on my own, buddy I don't need your help."[17]

I'm not sure I knew the difference between country music, which Malone (2002, 13) describes as "America's truest music," and outlaw country as a child. Outlaw country *was* country music so far as I knew until I was teenaged, at which point I saw a clearer link between southern rock and that brand of country music. Perhaps the hint of rhythm and blues through both constituent genres brought me to that point. Indeed, Jon Bernstein describes Americana as being a mix of roots music with more traditional styles of country and rhythm and blues music (pers. interview, March 17, 2021). Rather than splitting hairs, as social scientists tend, I shall point out that even what is conceived of as country music is rooted in folk (Kallen 1955). I

Robbie Fulks at the Bloodshot Records Backyard Barbeque in Nashville, Tennessee, on September 15, 2018. Courtesy Nick Barber.

will further resist the urge to provide the full lyrics to Robbie Fulks's "Countrier than Thou" (2005), which offers, "Down at the bar a-spinnin' Haggard, he wore a Johnny Reb tattoo. Overalls, he spat and swaggered. Lord, he was a Boston Jew."

Given that rock and roll is an outgrowth of rhythm and blues and that cowpunk is derived from country, there can be little doubt that all forms of Americana music are derived from folk, gospel, and the spirituals at the core. Therefore, I respectfully disagree with Malone (2002), who certainly does not lionize country music, before moving into my analysis. When considering the origins, Americana is the purest form of American music. These origins also underscore diversity, which points to the ability of Americana to speak to a broad audience. I do not lionize Americana, however. Stereotypes and regional cultural insularity, while often unintentional, prevent the genre from having a broader impact. Indeed, "raising hell with the hippies and the cowboys" may have a downside.[18]

Plan for the Book

Chapter 1 provides a theoretical foundation rooted in stereotyping. Specifically, Peffley, Hurwitz, and Sniderman (1997) find that when African Americans are presented as extremely stereotype-inconsistent, white Americans possessing strongly negative stereotypes of African Americans are likely to evaluate those African Americans far more positively. This research then posits that exposure to Americana music generally and racialized messages in this music more specifically will result in more positive evaluations of African Americans, immigrants, and the LGBTQ+ community than similar messages presented in rap music (i.e., the stereotype-confirming genre). This leads to directly addressing the connection between Americana music and race through a lyrical analysis that includes nominated music for Americana Music Association awards between 2002 (the first year of the Americana Music Awards) and 2021. Chapter 2 then looks to the lyrical analysis as a springboard to defining the musical genre based on thematic content, use of narrative, and presence of an artist best characterized as a singer-songwriter.

With Americana defined, chapter 3 moves forward by examining artists' thoughts and contributions. While not randomly selected, the twenty-three artists included in this study represent different constituent genres, a wide age range, differing educational backgrounds, and different geographic regions of the United States. They even include international artists playing in this space. Common themes established in artist interviews are the importance of narrative, deep contemplation and observation, and the listening environment.

Chapter 4 addresses the culture surrounding the Americana audience. This audience is, in some ways, as diverse as the genre and artists. Artists tend to define their audiences as representing varied occupational, regional, and socioeconomic backgrounds. However, there appears to be less racial diversity and some homogeneity of left-leaning political ideology. Indeed, music journalist and research editor for *Rolling Stone* Jon Bernstein characterizes the Americana audience as the "NPR crowd" (pers. interview, March 17, 2021).

Chapter 5 details the sample receiving varied experimental treatments, some of which contain Americana music. This chapter also elucidates the nature of the treatments and provides quantitative findings that point to exposure to Americana music often relating to more positive evaluations of minority groups, such as African Americans, immigrants, and the LGBTQ+ community. The chapter highlights the importance of identifying with Americana as well as the nuances of the findings, which suggest that care should be taken in unpacking the impact of this music.

Finally, the conclusion addresses the broader implications of the study, which include the need to further dissect the role of women in this musical space and the need to view Americana as a culture rather than a format or genre. I further ask whether a hypothetical increase in popularity of/exposure to Americana music, broadly defined, would dilute the impact of the inclusivity and tolerance provided in the music.

›››››› 1 ‹‹‹‹‹‹ THE FIRST VERSE

"Ronnie and Neil" (2001) by the Drive-By Truckers and Darrell Scott's "You'll Never Leave Harlan Alive" (1997) force the listener to consider both personal and societal struggles through rich narrative, which necessarily involves a consideration of rural America, race, and often poverty. Drive-By Truckers front man Patterson Hood begins his tribute to a key founding member of the southern rock band Lynyrd Skynyrd and Canadian-American singer-songwriter Neil Young with, "Church blew up in Birmingham. Four little Black girls killed for no goddamn good reason. All this hate and violence can't come to no good end. . . . Meanwhile in north Alabama Aretha Franklin comes to town to record that sweet soul music, to get that Muscle Shoals sound." Alternatively, Darrell Scott sings of southeastern Kentucky where the southern Appalachian coal miner is essentially trapped underground, "But the times got hard and tobacco wasn't selling. And old Granddad knew what he'd do to survive. He went and dug for Harlan coal and sent the money back to Grandma. But, he never made it out of Harlan alive."

A cursory reading of the lyrics would not give the impression that the two songs possess commonalities. Nevertheless, they share the label Americana and collectively illustrate key themes in Americana music—region, agriculture, spirituality and religion, life challenges, social awareness, and narrative.

The prominence of these narratives should not negate the role of race, as addressed at the onset of "Ronnie and Neil," in Americana music. As illustrated in the previous chapter, music and artists in this space possess deep roots across the United States, diversity in racial origins, and social awareness in messages. Nevertheless, the genre, at least as it appears from the outside, is dominated by white performers, songwriters, and instrumentalists. Further, the perceived focus on "outlaw country" often leaves outsiders ignoring the African American influences and presuming that country and southern rock dominate the genre. In turn, this chapter considers whether the medium could transmit progressive messages to typically unsusceptible audiences. This leads to the presentation of stereotyping as the theoretical foundation.

The chapter then moves to discussing the framework of the lyrical analysis. This framework considers demographic characteristics of the artists, themes addressed in lyrical content, and narrative framing using albums and artists nominated by the Americana Music Association as the sample. Prior to moving forward from this point, however, the reader is cautioned that familiarity and awareness relating to roots music are not synonymous. Individuals may hold the stereotypes relating to music labeled as Americana without having a high degree of familiarity with that music. Indeed, the ability of stereotypes to impact unfamiliar audiences is key in this analysis.

Theoretical Foundation

It's one thing to say music has diverse origins and messages. It's quite another to say that the industry, however conceived, takes measures to institutionalize diversity. Aengus Finnan suggests that while artist messaging and diversity are important, the artists can only do so much—venue owners, staff, etc. matter (pers. interview, May 18, 2020). Regardless of whether the person on stage conveys an inclusive message and/or represents a specific segment of the population, audiences are aware of their experiences in the culture. These experiences may be real or imagined, but that doesn't leave them less potent. For example, John Paul White, who delights in the diversity of his fan base and perceives his audience to be more progressive, reports being regularly approached by African American women following his show that tell him, "'I'm your one Black fan.' I'm like, 'No you're not, but you all seem to think this'" (pers. interview, May 10, 2021). Certainly this type of reaction could apply to the culture surrounding the music as well as the artists. Indeed, Bernstein reports that he's met a number of individuals who identify as fans of Americana broadly as much as fans of given artists (pers. interview, March 17, 2021).

John Paul White at the Beale Street Music Festival in Memphis, Tennessee, on May 6, 2017. Courtesy Maggie Mitchell.

Nevertheless, the artists are the most prominent faces of the culture, and they craft the messages. For example, when Gubitz and Avant (2020) consider the impact of diversity initiatives in the entertainment industry, their instrument does not vary the race of the secondary characters, it varies the race of the lead—in this case, Captain America. Their experiment speculated about replacing the white male lead in the popular *Captain America* film series with specific actors (both Black and white) versus vague language, or "cheap talk," pointing to a diversity initiative in filling the role, and concluded that "paying lip service to hiring practices is not enough to actually change attitudes and there must be action that follows the verbal commitment" (Gubitz and Avant 2020, 697–698).

I do not argue here that artist diversity does not matter or that "cheap talk"—in this case lyrical content reflecting diversity—replaces the need for diversity in artists and the broader Americana community. Rather, I suggest that the stereotypical views of Americana artists (i.e., white hippies and cowboys) may serve to promote a message of diversity in typically message-resistant audiences. In other words, understanding the impact of Americana music on political attitudes generally and racial attitudes specifically requires questioning with whom the stereotypical images of the artists resonate as well as the negative repercussions of the stereotypes. To that end, while stereotypes reinforce cultural insularity, that reinforcement may create a comfortable space for racially resentful consumers to receive messages they are predisposed to reject. More simply, those that potentially identify with the hippies and the cowboys from outside of the musical space may be tricked into processing the message. In turn, stereotypes may serve as a deterrent to some minority groups while serving as a vehicle to impart a message of diversity to those who might need to receive it most.

Walter Lippmann (1922, 11) stated, "The analyst of public opinion must begin then, by recognizing the triangular relationship between the scene of action, the human picture of that scene, and the human response to that picture working itself out upon the scene of action." That "human picture" is, of course, based on life experiences—however well-informed or ill-informed. The "pictures in our heads" that Lippmann describes allow people to make sense of the world around them, often in ways that may seem nonsensical to others. They are, in common parlance, stereotypes.

Scientific American featured an article by George Cadwallader Blayney in 1850 that discussed the process of "stereotyping." Blayney (1850) was not referring to a mental construct or process, however. He was referring to a physical process in which a pre-made metal sheet would be used to repeatedly print the same image of numerals, letters, etc. A social psychological approach to stereotyping, as we more commonly conceive it, is not unlike the physical printing Blayney described. Stereotypes are cognitive shortcuts that allow individuals, based on their own experiences (and their own interpretations of those experiences) to make sense of the environment. They are then mental imprints that are routinely used over time rather than physical printing that is reproduced in relatively rapid succession.

Stereotypes represent a theory-driven approach to information processing, relying on existing information that is not necessarily connected to real personal experience when making judgments. When one encounters stereotype-inconsistent information, this theory implies that effort will be made to force the contrary information to somehow fit with the stereotype (e.g., Hamilton and Sherman 1994). This type of information processing is often contrasted with a more data-driven approach that suggests individuals consider individuating information. In the case of music, as examined here, one might see Americana artists as white, but it is difficult to argue Keb' Mo's place in this space as an African American man who has recorded with the likes of Roseanne Cash and Old Crow Medicine Show and received the Americana Music Association's 2021 Lifetime Achievement Award for Performance.[1]

Keb' Mo', like other minority artists, may be perceived as stereotype-inconsistent with Americana music. Stereotype-inconsistency (or stereotype-incongruence) can have a powerful impact, however. Peffley, Hurwitz, and Sniderman (1997) illustrate this power by varying the race of targets in experimental treatments of welfare and crime. Why welfare and crime? These policy areas are known to be racially coded, meaning that the evocation of the terms immediately elicit mental images of African Americans as the key demographic impacted (e.g., Gilens 1996; 1999; Hurwitz and Peffley 2005; Peffley and Hurwitz 2002; Valentino 1999).[2] For whites with negative stereotypes of Blacks, opposition to welfare and crime can then fuel their evaluations without giving the appearance of overt racism—this is the primary thesis of symbolic racism (e.g., Sears 1988), subtle racism (e.g., Pettigrew and Meertens 1995), modern racism (e.g., McConahay 1986), and color-blind racism (e.g., Bonilla-Silva 2003).[3] In other words, for these whites, their attitudes are not about racial resentment. Rather, these attitudes are about the violation of closely held morals and ideals. As noted dramatically by Bonilla-Silva in the title of his 2003 investigation of color-blind racism, falling back on cultural explanations gives the appearance of "racism without racists."[4]

Returning to the Peffley, Hurwitz, and Sniderman (1997) analysis, whites with negative stereotypes of Blacks will "bend over backwards" in their evaluations of stereotype-inconsistent targets. In other words, when Black targets are presented as hardworking, well-behaved, and unlikely to use foul language, the whites with preexisting negative views of African Americans evaluated Black targets very positively.

This same logic can be applied to music. For those whites holding negative views of African Americans, exposure to music seen as stereotypically Black (e.g., rap) will reinforce those stereotypes and bias evaluations of African Americans generally and policies impacting Blacks more specifically. Alternatively, these same whites will be far more positive in their evaluations of African Americans and related policies when exposed to Americana music—a stereotype-disconfirming medium.

But This Is Music

A logical question that follows the use of stereotype-incongruence as a theoretical framework is, "Can this really be applied to music?" A growing literature examines the impact of entertainment media, from less obvious political messaging in major motion pictures (e.g., Gierzynski 2018; Gubitz and Avant 2020), fantasy series such as *Game of Thrones* (e.g., Gierzynski 2018), and crime dramas (e.g., Holbrook and Hill 2006) to more overt political messaging in specific programming, such as *House of Cards* and *The Colbert Report* (e.g., Gierzynski 2018). J. K. Rowling's popular *Harry Potter* series, for example, has inspired research that suggests fans of the fantasy narrative are more tolerant and less authoritarian than nonfans (Gierzynski 2013), and there is an association between consumption of the series and opposition to Donald Trump (Mutz 2016).

The obvious rub with considering entertainment programming, whether movies, serials, or music, as I investigate here, is selective exposure. More specifically, individuals choose entertainment programming with which they already agree, leaving the impact of exposure limited to reinforcement at best. Gierzynksi (2018) rebuffs this notion by pointing to audiences seeking out fictional programming to be entertained rather than to facilitate political development. Combining entertainment with narrative transportation enhances emotional investment (Gierzynski 2018).

Narrative transportation theory explains the emotional investment of the traveler (i.e., a consumer of storytelling) who "loses access to some real-world facts in favor of accepting the narrative world that the author has created. This loss of access may occur on a physical level—a transported reader may not notice others entering the room, for example—or, more importantly, on a psychological level, a subjective distancing from reality" (Green and Brock 2000, 702). More succinctly, the entirety of transported consumers' mental capacities are focused on the story (Fitzgerald and Green 2017). This process can lead to belief change relating to identification with a given story's protagonist and adopting attitudes related to dominant themes in the work.[5] Such identification with characters and themes is enhanced by the consumer's ability to see themself as an actor in the narrative (see Seliman and Larson 1989). The extension of entertainment and narrative transportation to music is evident, as music is clearly an entertainment medium that often incorporates storytelling. Thus, music could be seen as impacting political attitudes.

Further, extant research establishes that rap music impacts political attitudes (Bonnette 2015; Spence 2011). While this literature does in part support the reinforcement of existing beliefs (Spence 2011), it nevertheless illustrates the ability of music to serve as a political tool. Bonnette's (2015) analysis serves to underscore this point through the use of a survey experiment where the stimulus varied from political rap and nonpolitical rap to pop music. Those exposed to political rap were more likely to support Black nationalism than those exposed to other forms of music.

While Bonnette's (2015) analysis and design illustrate the ability of rap music to impact political attitudes, the focus of the analysis is Black political attitudes. This is a pivotal distinction between that analysis and the one presented here. Bonnette (2015) did not look to a stereotype-disconfirming medium. Care must be taken in understanding and applying stereotype-incongruence as a framework, however. Regarding understanding, Peffley, Hurwitz, and Sniderman (1997) consider attitudes toward policies and speculate that whites with negative views of Blacks go to the extremes to positively evaluate stereotype-inconsistent Black targets because that action allows them to hold their stereotypes of Blacks intact. More specifically, pristine Black targets are the exception (e.g., "this Black is different"), flawed Blacks are the rule (e.g., "most Blacks are lazy, hostile, and foul-mouthed"). If this is the case, the outcome is less about positively evaluating Blacks and more about the preservation of their stereotype.

The application here is different, and that is key. Crime and welfare are racially coded to reflect African Americans as the targets and beneficiaries, respectively. Americana music is stereotypically white. The exposure to "white music"—regardless of the accuracy of the stereotype—begins from a mental state of neutrality or positivity to those whites with negative stereotypes of Blacks rather than beginning from a place of negativity, as opposed to rap music, which could elicit negative racial stereotypes from the onset of exposure.[6] Further, unless one possesses a great deal of familiarity with this genre, it may not be conceived as overtly political. Indeed one could argue that the medium, while often involving socially aware artists and lyrics, does not typically tackle overt partisan politics.

In sum, positive narrative transportation about African Americans via Americana music—a stereotypically white medium—allows whites with negative preconceptions of African Americans to challenge the stereotype by creating an emotional connection without overtly forcing them to think about political impact or beginning from a place of negativity. Thus, "bending over backwards" in this application is not necessarily done in the attempt to preserve the stereotype.

The stereotype-incongruence hypothesis is supported empirically through the application of a survey-based experiment. These results are presented in chapter 5. Prior to delving deeply into the experimental design and results, however, a better understanding of musical content is necessary. After all, while even a cursory historical consideration of musical roots reveals diversity, that does not necessarily equate to contemporary artists and lyrics reflecting diversity in a meaningful way.

Artist Demographic Assessment

The preceding theoretical development suggests an incongruence for some people between message and artist and alternate audience stereotypical sketch of artist and message. While the history presented in the introduction supports theoretical expectations, a look at those artists nominated by the Americana Music Association for Song of the Year, Album of the Year, and Artist of the Year from 2002 to 2021 (as well as other artist-centered awards) illustrates the preponderance of heterosexual white male artists. That dominance clearly reinforces the hippie and/or cowboy stereotype.

Certainly, artists other than those nominated for Americana Music Association awards are prominent in this space. In fact, artists such as Guy Clark and Townes Van Zandt were writing and performing long before *Honky Tonk Amnesia* was conceived, and Van Zandt died five years prior to the first Americana Music Association awards ceremony. Nevertheless, the diversity of constituent genres requires a decision-rule that takes constituent genre into consideration. Utilizing Americana Music Association nominations to identify relevant music and artists permits the inclusion of artists from across constituent genres without taking a more overtly biased approach, such as radio playlists, audio streaming service statistics (e.g., Pandora and Spotify), YouTube likes, or album sales. There is some discrepancy between artists nominated for Song of the Year or Album of the Year and those nominated for Artist/Duo/Group of the Year, Emerging Act of the Year, Achievement in Songwriting, Achievement in Instrumental, and Achievement in Performance, however.[7] For this reason, descriptive information related to each is presented separately below (i.e., Song of the Year nominations, Album of the Year nominations, and total nominations across seven categories specifying artists).

There are eighty-five observations of Song of the Year by sixty artists.[8] Most artists were nominated only once, but five artists stand out as having more than two nominations. Lucinda Williams, Steve Earle, and Hayes Carll each received three nominations in this category, while Rodney Crowell received four nominations for Song of the Year. Crowell won twice. Jason Isbell has the most nominations for Song of the Year with five. He has, at the date of writing, won four times.

There are eighty-three nominations for Album of the Year; however, only eighty-one are considered here, given that two are tribute albums featuring a myriad of artists.[9] Of the eighty-one nominations considered, there are sixty artists. Jason Isbell is easily the most-nominated artist in this category, having received a total of six nominations for both his solo work and for Jason Isbell and the 400 Unit.

Utilizing nominations and wins for Artist of the Year, Instrumentalist of the Year, Emerging Act of the Year, Duo/Group of the Year, Lifetime Achievement in Songwriting, Lifetime Achievement in Performance, and Lifetime Achievement in Instrumental results in significantly more observations. There are 376 observations in these seven categories during the nineteen year period of the Americana Music Awards covered in this analysis. Further, there are a total of 224 artists represented.[10]

White heterosexual men constitute well over half (56.47 percent, or 48 observations) of those artists nominated for Song of the Year by the Americana Music Association.[11] White heterosexual women were nominated twenty-five times (29.41 percent) in this category. Duos/groups consisting of both white heterosexual men and white heterosexual women were nominated six times (7.06 percent). Sequentially, only five nominations for Song of the Year involved openly lesbian artists.[12] There have been no openly gay male artists nominated for Song of the Year by the Americana Music Association. There is scant racial/ethnic diversity in Song of the Year nominations from 2002 to 2021. Brittany Howard, an openly gay African American woman who is also a member of Alabama Shakes, was the lone African American nominee until 2021, when two African American women, Amythyst Kiah (another open lesbian) and Valerie June received Song of the Year nominations. Although June is heterosexual, chart 1.1 includes all racial/ethnic minority artists nominated for Song of the Year with LGBTQ+ artists for ease of presentation.

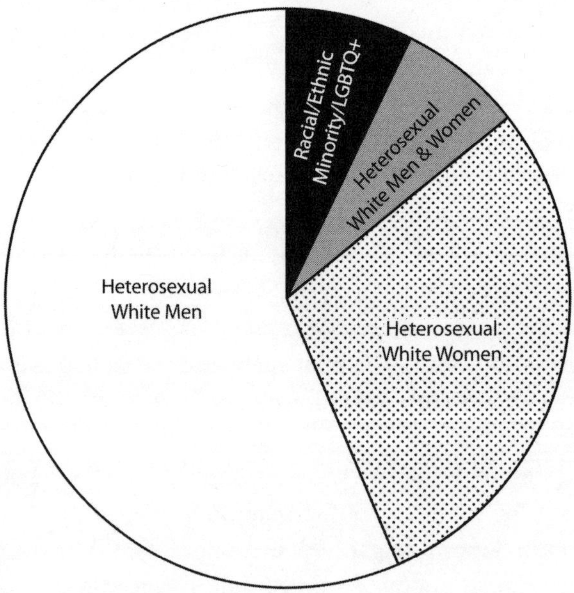

Chart 1.1. Americana Music Association Song of the Year Nominations by Race and Sexual Orientation

White heterosexual men also comprise more than half of the artists nominated for Album of the Year, though this prevalence is slightly less evident when compared to Song of the Year nominations (i.e., 51.81 percent nominated for Album of the Year compared to >56 percent nominated for Song of the Year). Heterosexual white women constitute approximately 27 percent of Album of the Year nominations, while 8.43 percent of the nominations were for a combination of white heterosexual men and women. Thus, approximately 13 percent of these nominations were for racial/ethnic and/or LGBTQ+ artists (this includes nominations for six heterosexual racial/ethnic minority artists, one for an LGBTQ+ racial/ethnic minority artist, three for white LGBTQ+ artists, and one for a group consisting of heterosexual and LGBTQ+ artists). All minority artists are grouped together for ease of interpretation in chart 1.2.

The dominance of white heterosexual men is slightly more pronounced when looking across all seven categories. This demographic represents 56.8 percent of the artists nominated across the seven categories. Only one Americana Music Association-nominated white male performer, Aaron Lee Tasjan, identifies as nonheterosexual (Tasjan identifies as bisexual).[13]

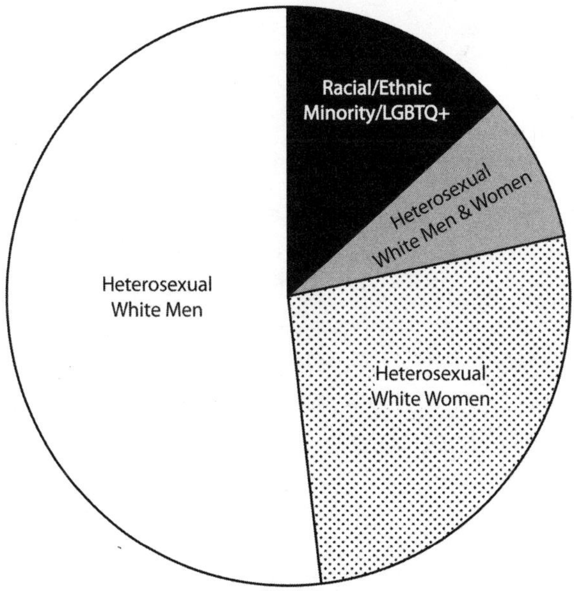

Chart 1.2. American Music Association Album of the Year Nominations by Race and Sexual Orientation

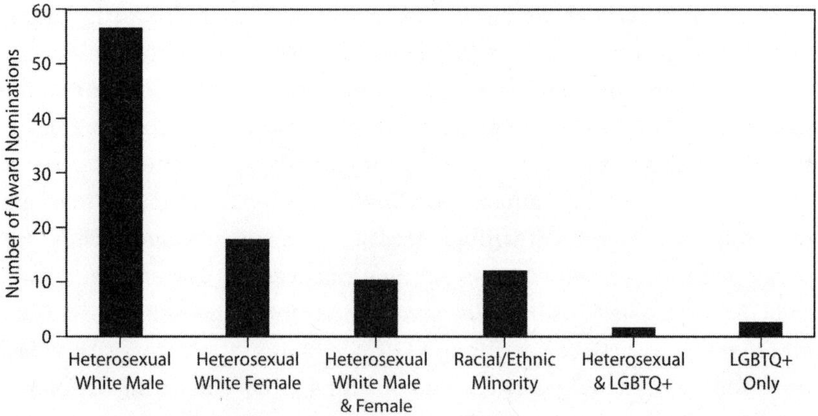

Chart 1.3. Americana Music Association Awards Nominations (7 Categories Combined) by Race/Ethnicity, Gender, Sexual Orientation

Heterosexual white women constitute the next largest portion of the group at 17.87 percent. Duos/groups consisting of heterosexual white men and heterosexual white women comprise 10.67 percent of performers nominated across the seven categories.

Artists that can be characterized as racial/ethnic minorities make up 12 percent of the nominations across the seven categories considered here.[14] Alternatively, 2.93 percent (or 18 observations) of those performers nominated across the categories are openly LGBTQ+ without performing with a nonheterosexual artist. Brandi Carlile constitutes nearly half of this group with four nominations. This figure is slightly misleading, however. An additional 1.87 percent of those nominated are groups featuring both heterosexual and homosexual performers (i.e., Alabama Shakes, The Highwomen, and Our Native Daughters). Brandi Carlile is notably also a member of The Highwomen, suggesting she is presently the most successful LGBTQ+ artist in Americana, if associated awards are utilized as a measure for determining degree of success.. Chart 1.3 allows for overlapping group memberships.

Disparity in sexual orientation notwithstanding, the prevalence of white artists is notable considering the racial/ethnic diversity historically present in Americana's constituent subgenres. Eighty-eight percent of nominated artists are white. In fact, no non-white artist was nominated for these seven categories during the first eight years of the Americana Music Awards. Fur-

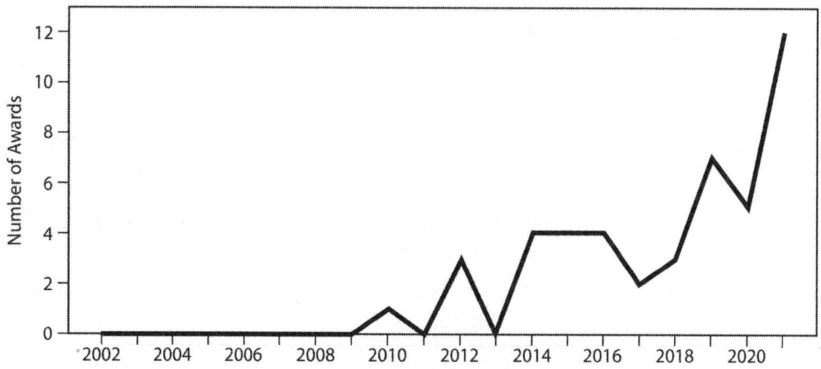

Graph 1.1. Americana Music Association Awards Racial/Ethnic Growth (7 Categories Combined)

ther, only four nominations in these categories featured non-whites from 2002 to 2013. Since this time, however, non-white artists have received multiple nominations each year, with a low of two in 2017 and a high of twelve in 2021 (see graph 1.1).

Assessing descriptive representation among artists is important. Not only does the dominance of heterosexual white men reinforce existing stereotypes, but an in-depth consideration of nominated artists also illustrates that diversity is growing across the genre. Notably, the Americana Music Association focused on diversity in 2021 and gave the appearance of minority domination at the Americana Music Awards. Brandi Carlile was named Artist of the Year, Black Pumas, which features one Black and one white artist, was named Duo/Group of the Year, and Charley Crockett, of multicultural descent, was named Emerging Act of the Year.[15] Furthermore, Legacy and Lifetime Achievement Awards were dominated by racial/ethnic minorities, including recognition of the Fisk Jubilee Singers, who are an African American a cappella ensemble associated with Fisk University, a Historically Black University.[16]

Despite the growing representation of minorities in Americana, descriptive representation among artists is only one piece of this puzzle. Determining the surface messaging in song and album titles as well as the deeper messaging present in lyrics is pivotal. To this end, white and/or heterosexual artists can provide substantive representation.

Thematic Content Analysis Framework

In order to deconstruct lyrics, song titles, and album titles thematically, I devised a coding instrument. The instrument allowed for both inductive and deductive coding. More specifically, using the historical development of the various constituent genres as a starting point, I began the process anticipating that region/agriculture, religion/spirituality, and politics/social awareness would be common themes in this space.

Concurrently using an inductive approach guided me to two additional prevalent themes—struggle/life challenges and the use of narrative given the unexpected volume of nominated music failing to incorporate narrative. While romantic love is a dominant thematic element, I do not consider it in this analysis unless it is related to another theme (e.g., struggle resulting from loss of love) because romantic love is not unique across musical genres.

Songs, song titles, and album titles are coded as having a primary focus in one of these themes (aside from narrative, which is dichotomous) if terms related to the individual themes are mentioned twice or more. A single reference is considered a secondary focus. While search terms and relevant Albums/Songs of the Year are presented in the tables below for descriptive purposes, the following chapter provides a more thorough consideration of the content analysis.

Region and agriculture represent a single theme. Agriculture, both farming and ranching, is intrinsically tied to states, communities, and regions. Therefore, terms that address nature, crops, and livestock fall into this category in the same manner as terms that reflect regions, states, and more specific geographic locations, such as specific cities, bodies of water, mountain ranges, etc. Column 1 in table 1.1 features search terms associated with region and agriculture, while column 2 features titles of nominated albums containing the relevant terms. Likewise, column 3 features titles of nominated songs.

Religion and spirituality are not synonymous, but they are related concepts and occupy the same thematic space in this research. Terms referencing religiosity relating to religious figures, places of worship, religious activity, religious paraphernalia, etc., are included, as are terms that address death and the afterlife. Table 1.2 presents key search terms and titles of Albums and Songs of the Year.

Like religion and spirituality, politics and social awareness are distinct but very much related concepts. Therefore, I consider terms that repre-

Table 1.1. Region and Agriculture

Search Terms	*Nominated Album Titles (Artist, Year)*	*Nominated Song Titles (Artist, Year)*
Agriculture	*Cuttin' Grass, Vol. 1* (Sturgill Simpson, 2021)	"Dime Store Cowboy" (Kasey Musgraves, 2016)
Bodies of Water (e.g., ocean)	*World on the Ground* (Sarah Jarosz, 2021)	"The River and the Thread" (Roseanne Cash, 2014)
Cities/Towns (e.g., Nashville)	*Country Squire* (Tyler Childers, 2020)	"Birmingham" (Shovels & Rope, 2013)
Country	*The Tree* (Lori McKenna, 2019)	"Alabama Pines" (Jason Isbell, 2012)
Farm/Farming	*The Tree of Forgiveness* (John Prine, 2019)	"Harlem River Blues" (Justin Townes Earle, 2011)
Livestock (e.g., cows)	*The Nashville Sound* (Jason Isbell & the 400 Unit, 2018)	"Country Love" (The Gourds, 2009)
Ranch/Ranching	*Southeastern* (Jason Isbell, 2014)	"Poor Old Dirt Farmer" (Levon Helm, 2008)
Regions (e.g., South, Appalachia)	*The River and the Thread* (Roseanne Cash, 2014)	"Portland, Oregon" (Loretta Lynn, 2004)
Terms associated with Farming (e.g., barn, tractor)	*From the Ground Up* (John Fullbright, 2013)	
Terms addressing Nature (e.g., earth, grass, ground, dirt, tree, harvest)	*The Harrow and the Harvest* (Gillian Welch, 2012)	
Terms associated with Ranching (e.g., cowboy, ranch)	*Harlem River Blues* (Justin Townes Earle, 2011)	
	Dirt Farmer (Levon Helm, 2008)	
	West (Lucinda Williams, 2007)	
	Van Lear Rose (Loretta Lynn, 2004)	

sent partisan politics (e.g., Democrat and Republican) as well as terms that reflect policies, public office, the military, and social issues more broadly. Table 1.3 presents key search terms and titles of Albums and Songs of the Year.

Life challenges represent a dominant theme in Americana music. Unlike region/agriculture, religion/spirituality, and politics/social awareness,

Table 1.2. Religion and Spirituality

Search Terms	*Nominated Album Titles (Artist, Year)*	*Nominated Song Titles (Artist, Year)*
Afterlife (incl. related references)	*Rifles and Rosary Beads* (Mary Gauthier, 2018)	"Thoughts and Prayers" (Drive-By Truckers, 2020)
Bless/Blessed/Blessing	*Down Where the Spirit Meets the Bone* (Lucinda Williams, 2015)	"Dearly Departed" (Shakey Graves, 2015)
Devoted/Devotion	*O' Be Joyful* (Shovels & Rope, 2013)	"Downtown Church" (Patty Griffin, 2010)
Eternity	*I'll Never Get Out of This World Alive* (Steve Earle, 2012)	"She Left Me for Jesus" (Hayes Carll, 2008)
Faith	*Here We Rest* (Jason Isbell & the 400 Unit, 2012)	"Heavenly Day" (Patty Griffin, 2007)
Fate	*Blessed* (Lucinda Williams, 2011)	"Mercy Now" (Mary Gauthier, 2005)
Heaven/Heavenly	*Soul's Chapel* (Marty Stuart & His Fabulous Superlatives, 2006)	"Come to Jesus" (Mindy Smith, 2004)
Holy	*Mercy Now* (Mary GTuthier, 2005)	"Fate's Right Hand" (Rodney Crowell, 2004)
Judgment	*United Universal House of Prayer* (Buddy Miller, 2005)	"Righteously" (Lucinda Williams, 2003)
Mercy/Merciful	*Fate's Right Hand* (Rodney Crowell, 2004)	
Places of Worship (e.g., church, chapel)		
Pray/Prayer		
Religion		
Religious Artifacts/Paraphernalia		
Religious Figures (e.g., Jesus)		
Righteous/Righteously		
Savior		
Spirit		
Soul		
Titles reflecting/reminiscent of Hymns		

struggle and strife are not easily conveyed with singular terms. Rather, a consideration of the totality of song lyrics is pivotal in discerning struggle. In turn, I do not address struggle relating to album or song titles. I similarly do not provide search terms because each nominated song was analyzed individually to determine whether this theme was present.

Table 1.3. Politics and Social Awareness

Search Terms	*Nominated Album Titles (Artist, Year)*	*Nominated Song Titles (Artist, Year)*
American/Americans	*All American Made* (Margo Price, 2008)	"A Long Violent History" (Tyler Childers, 2021)
Democrats	*Rifles and Rosary Beads* (Mary Gauthier, 2018)	"Black Myself" (Amythyst Kiah, 2021)
Free/Freedom	*American Band* (Drive-By Truckers, 2017)	"KMAG YOYO" (Hayes Carll, 2011)
Liberty	*Freedom Highway* (Rhiannon Giddens, 2017)	"It Takes Balls to Be a Woman" (Elizabeth Cook, 2007)
Names of Offices/ Office Holders (e.g., President, Bush)	*A Sailor's Guide to Earth* (Sturgill Simpson, 2017)	"The Revolution Starts . . . Now" (Steve Earle, 2005)
Terms related to Artillery/ Ammunition (e.g., bullet, rifle)	*Something More than Free* (Jason Isbell, 2016)	
Terms related to the Military (e.g., AWOL, Navy, soldier)	*And the War Came* (Shakey Graves, 2015)	
Terms related to Political Institutions (e.g., Congress)	*A. Enlightenment B. Endarkenment (Hint: There is no C.)* (Ray Wylie Hubbard, 2010)	
Terms related to Race/ Ethnicity (somewhat inductive)	*The Revolution Starts . . . Now* (Steve Earle, 2005)	
Terms related to Social Awareness (somewhat inductive)	*American IV: The Man Comes Around* (Johnny Cash, 2003)	
Republican		
Revolution/ Revolutionary		
Vote/Voting		
War/Warfare		

Narrative, which many of the artists interviewed for this piece contend is critical and which Gierzynski's (2018) study suggests is key in facilitating political effects, is also assessed individually without key search terms. In order to determine if a story unfolds, one must listen to the song. Hence, narrative and life challenges are addressed with precision in chapter 2, which evaluates lyrics based on the content analysis elucidated here en route to establishing a framework for a more thorough definition of Americana beyond "American roots music."

Summary

This chapter has extended and evolved the discussion of stereotypical views of Americana artists presented in the introduction into a theoretical foundation based in stereotype-incongruence. The chapter has also presented descriptive statistics based on Americana Music Association award nominations, which underscore the dominance of white heterosexual men in this musical space while also noting growing racial/ethnic and LGBTQ+ diversity. Likewise, the ability of entertainment media generally and music specifically to impact political attitudes has been addressed.

Prior to exploring the results of the experimental analysis, however, the lyrics, artists, and culture deserve greater consideration. Simply because white heterosexual men are prevalent does not mean that the genre fails to promote inclusivity. Indeed, the historical and theoretical development presented here and in the previous chapter point to a preponderance of socially aware lyrics and a general embracing of diversity. It is the very combination of the message of inclusivity and the historical prominence of heterosexual white men in this space that fosters the ability of this music to impact political attitudes in message-resistant audiences.

»»»»»» 2 «««««««

THE MUSIC

Hayes Carll and Darrell Scott evoke easily identifiable images of musicians in "For the Sake of the Song" (2016). "And there's the mystic, there's the legend, and there's the best that's ever been. And there's the voice of a generation who wants to pass this way again. And there's record deals and trained seals, and puppets on a string. And they're all just trying to figure out what makes the caged bird sing." Aside from the Maya Angelou reference that very clearly evokes powerful racial imagery, perhaps the gravel in Carll's voice as he paints caricatures of artists so vivid that audiences can attach specific names and faces is a poignant aspect of the song.[1] But musical interpretation is often left to the listener, and "For the Sake of the Song" allows audiences to reach the obvious conundrum with Americana music that's reminiscent of the diversity among the artists Carll and Scott address—a concise definition is elusive.

American roots music is comprised of several constituent genres that are associated with different regions, messages, cultures, and even instruments. To that end, a lyric from Julie Miller's 2002 "Midnight and Lonesome" may characterize the Americana format: "There's a sound with no name where a faraway train cries like an unloved child."[2] This "unnamed" sound potentially leaves consumers tempted to fall back on Potter Stewart's 1964 approach to hardcore pornography when attempting to define the Americana format, "I shall not today attempt further to define . . . and perhaps I could never succeed in intelligibly doing so. But I know it when I see it."[3] Nevertheless, an attempt must be made to identify common characteristics of Americana despite the difficulty in pinpointing a precise definition aside from "American roots music." Absent such an attempt, scholars can neither adequately study the music that comprises the format nor systematically study the effects. In turn, this chapter identifies those common characteristics by looking to the history and the findings of the content analysis of Americana Music Association-nominated music presented in the previous chapters as well as the thoughts of music journalists. In turn, I arrive at a scheme of identifying music associated with the Americana format, which hinges on constituent genre and songwriting, that is used in the following chapters. To that end, lyrical quotations presented throughout this study meet the definition of Americana music.

Constituent Genres

The first step in defining Americana is to restate the constituent genres of music developed in and/or associated strongly with the United States. Per the historical evolution addressed in the previous chapters, several constituent genres of American roots music exist. Specific constituent genres include (but aren't limited to) bluegrass, blues, country, cowpunk, folk, gospel, jazz, rock and roll, rockabilly, and southern rock. Americana has become a blanket term to cover music that fits comfortably into each of these genres or incorporates elements from a combination of them. Indeed, Slaid Cleaves says that "if [Americana] is innovative, it's only innovative in the way it mixes folk, country, blues, gospel" (pers. interview, February 24, 2021). To that end, the first step in characterizing Americana music is to establish whether a given song or artist can be seen as fitting into one or more of these constituent genres.

Music from the Heartland

Author and music journalist Lee David Zimmerman's characterization of Americana as "music from the heartland," while apt given the regional origins and development of constituent genres, necessitates operationalizing heartland (pers. interview, February 11, 2021). Political scientists may refer to the heartland as rural America, the southern and midwestern regions of the United States, regions of the country dependent on agriculture generally (or farming and/or ranching specifically), "fly-over states," and/or "red states." The latter characterization is particularly notable, given that "red states" refers to those states that tend to vote for Republican candidates at the federal level and that Americana music is often referred to as "country music for Democrats."[4]

Defining the American heartland can be nearly as difficult as defining Americana music. For instance, Berry (1980) considers trends in urbanization and counterurbanization in the United States, frequently evoking the heartland, without ever actually defining it. Perhaps this is because "heartland" may be presumed to simply be the geographic "heart" of the United States, as in noncoastal. This assumption would be short-sighted and limited, however.

Rural states and agricultural centers often exist in close proximity to the American coastlines. California and Texas provide fitting illustrations, as these states have lengthy coastlines and their economies are driven, in part, by agriculture. In fact, California has the highest crop production across the United States and Texas has the highest livestock production in the country.[5] Certainly, agriculture, much like rurality, region, and religion, relates to the American heartland. Therefore, I look to the aforementioned thematic elements of the heartland.

Region and agriculture occupy thematic and titular prominence in Americana music. Artists use related terms in band names (e.g., Southern Culture on the Skids), in album titles (e.g., *Southern Rock Opera* and *The Dirty South,* 2001 and 2004 Drive-By Truckers albums, respectively), explicitly in song titles (e.g., "Alabama at Night" [2016] by Robbie Fulks, "Farm Fresh Onions" [2003] by Robert Earl Keen, and "Oklahoma Stars" [2017] by the Turnpike Troubadours), and implicitly in song titles (e.g., Tim O'Brien's "Cornbread Nation" [2005]).

Corb Lund even defines his specific constituent genre, and titles his 2020 album *Agricultural Tragic.* While Lund is an international artist, the album addresses ranching, horse riding, hunting, and a general sense of rurality. Each of these concepts is unavoidably related to the American heartland and Americana music, and conveys a sense of the culture contributing to the music. For example, Lund pays homage to his mother in the 2020 *Agricultural Tragic* piece "Never Not Had Horses." "Without some kind of cavvy 'round, she don't know who she is. She grew up trailin' cattle in the Rockies as a kid. She rode to a one room schoolhouse, learned her letters pass or fail. And each day her greatest teacher was just outside, tied to the rails."

The Turnpike Troubadours frequently evoke images of farms, ranches, and hunting in their music. Evan Felker tells the story of an elderly man meeting his demise in this type of setting: "There was square hay on the meadow, second cutting of the year. Well his summer work was over once they got the pasture cleared. They were drinking on the big bluff, across the river from the field. Well he walked up to the edge and threw a stone in and he kneeled. And he looked down at the water, he said 'boys I'm going in.' They were cheering when he jumped, but he did not come up again."[6] "The Bird Hunters" (2015) clearly conveys hunting in the title, but it also conveys rurality in the lyrics: "The country was cold with the sun westward sinking. It's good to be back in this place. With my hands around a Belgium made Browning, my mind on the lines of her face." The band further eloquently addresses rural Oklahoma and ranching in "Three Rivers Song" (2007): "So you best buy your permits and round up your cattle. If you're too proud to leave, you'll be too poor to stay. And remember the good times, back when you had 'em. Well you know Mr. Weyerhaeuser has the last say."

Region and rurality can be seen throughout Robbie Fulk's Grammy-nominated 2016 *Upland Stories*. Beyond the cues in album song titles, such as "Alabama at Night" and "Fare Thee Well, Carolina Gals," lyrics in these songs and others on the album reflect both midwestern and southern themes as well as roots music. For instance, Fulks sings of Virginia and North Carolina in "Aunt Peg's New Old Man." "They played dances, made the rounds. Galax to Rocky Mount. The tunes they knew no one could count. It was all in their heads and their hands." Further, Fulks specifically addresses region in "Fare Thee Well, Carolina Gals": "By luck I landed in the upper south. By God I gotta make my own way out. I should have read the signs by now. I should have heard the locusts buzzin'."

A consideration of the Americana Music Association's nominated Albums of the Year between 2002, the first year of the awards, and 2021 illustrates that album titles often include terms associated with regions (including states) and agriculture. Nearly 17 percent of these albums (fourteen of eighty-three) contain titles with terms depicting regions, nature, states, cities, rurality, farming, ranching, etc. Greater than 9 percent of the songs nominated for Song of the Year (eight of eighty-five) during this period also include such terms in the titles.[7]

The content analysis of the lyrics of nominated songs during this time frame reveals that greater than one-quarter of these songs (twenty-three of eighty-five) can be characterized as having a primary or secondary focus on region and/or agriculture. Of those, sixteen focus primarily on region and/or agriculture.

Songs specifically addressing region include the 2014 Best Song-winning "Cover Me Up," in which Jason Isbell sings of both a dam and a river in Tennessee: "So girl, hang your dress up to dry. We ain't leaving this room. 'Til Percy Priest breaks open wide and the river runs through. And carries this house on the Stones like a piece of driftwood." Similarly, agriculture is evoked when Levon Helm sings "Poor Old Dirt Farmer" (2007). The same can be said of the Americana all-female super group The Highwomen's 2019 award-wining "Crowded Table": "If we want a garden, we're gonna have to sow the seeds. Plant a little happiness. Let the roots run deep."[8]

Spirituality and Religion

Lucinda Williams's "Pineola" (1992) provides the perfect bridge from addressing geography to discussing spirituality with her raw account of loss in a southern town: "Born and raised in Pineola. His Mama believed in the Pentecost. She got the preacher to say some words so his soul would not be lost." While not the lone religion represented in Americana music, this Christian interpretation of spirituality can be seen in a great deal of American roots music, specifically that rooted in the gospel constituent genre.

The introduction explored the origins of American gospel music, which was pioneered by African Americans in the southern United States. It further addressed the evolution of country music as key in the development of what would come to be referred to as Americana music. The cultural and social impact of country music cannot be overstated, and neither can gospel's impact on contemporary Americana music.

Grimshaw's (2002) analysis of Gram Parsons, the posthumous recipient of the Americana Music Association's 2003 President's Award, illustrates the link between religion and American roots music. Parsons's approach to music, performance, and lifestyle can be seen as a blending of debauchery and devotion (Dawidoff 1997). This religiously devoted while often hard-living characterization can be made of many artists labeled or perceived as "country" and/or in the professional lineage of Johnny Cash, who is recognized as an icon in country and rockabilly (Grant 2006).

Despite the gospel and Christian connections, the distinction between religious and evangelical is key in establishing religion's place in Americana music. For evangelicals, the complexity of life can be reduced to simplistic answers and explanations, while for musicians such as Parsons life is hard and answers are seldom easy (Grimshaw 2002). In turn, country music, like gospel, often grapples with the ultimate dilemma of seeking redemption and salvation while often falling prey to worldly temptations.

Jason Isbell tackles this struggle with learning oneself and attempting to come to terms with religion in the 2015 Americana Music Association's Song of the Year, "24 Frames": "You thought God was an architect, now you know. He's something like a pipe bomb ready to blow. And everything you built that's all for show goes up in flames. In 24 frames."

It is precisely this type of introspection and contemplation that prolific country and Americana singer/songwriter Rodney Crowell sees as absent in contemporary country (pers. interview, March 3, 2021). Crowell, who achieved great success in popular country music, winning several awards by the Country Music Association as well as Grammy Awards, chose to walk away from mainstream success in order to develop what he sees as more contemplative, socially responsible, and meaningful music. Crowell, who embraces spirituality while jokingly referring to himself as a "Pentecostal Buddhist," admittedly takes religion to task in order to encourage greater understanding. "The evangelicals are arrogant.... How can you relate to your creator through a single lens?" In 2003's "Preaching to the Choir," Crowell begins, "My self importance is a God forsaken bore. I aim for heaven, but I wake up on the floor. I'd take up with the rattlesnakes to get my point across. And I'd argue with a parking brake to show 'em who's the boss. It's my intention to inspire instead I'm preachin' to the choir."

Religion, faith, spirituality, and related terminology is often used in titles of Americana albums and songs. Twelve percent of all albums nominated for the Americana Music Association's Album of the Year (ten of eighty-three) contain related terms. Similarly, greater than 10 percent of titles of songs nominated for Song of the Year (nine of eighty-five) include related terms.

Lyrical content addressing religion, faith, the afterlife, etc., can be seen in more than 42 percent of nominated songs (thirty-six of eighty-five) during this period. Nearly 42 percent of these songs (fifteen of thirty-six) can be said to have religion, faith, the afterlife, etc., as a primary focus. This should not be interpreted as Americana music encouraging a specific religious or faith-based message, however. Rather, religious focus can refer to the use of religious phrasing or terms, and the tone can vacillate from uplifting to critical. To illustrate, Gillian Welch and Dave Rawlings sing, "I want to reach that glory land. I want to shake my savior's hand, and I want to sing that rock and roll. I want to electrify my soul."[9] Alternatively, Patterson Hood warns, "They'll throw the bums all out, drain the swamp for real. Perp walk them down the capital steps and show them how it feels. Tramp the dirt down, Jesus, you can pray the rod they'll spare. Stick it up your ass with your useless thoughts and prayers," in the Drive-By Truckers 2020 response to mass school shootings.[10]

Hayes Carll takes yet another approach to religion in the 2008 Americana Music Association's Best Song winner. Humor is the foundation of "She Left Me for Jesus" as Carll declares, "She left me for Jesus, and that just ain't fair. She says that he's perfect. How could I compare? She says I should find him and I'll know peace at last. But if I ever find Jesus, I'm kicking his ass."[11]

Humor is on the surface of Todd Snider's "In the Beginning" (2012) as well, but Snider pushes the listener to think beyond the surface. This tale suggests that the origins of religion lie with a wealthy man devising a scheme to survive and maintain his possessions. "Well, the crowd just didn't know what to do. Nor could they prove what he said wasn't true. And since he had what everyone else thought they wanted, it seemed like a thing to do. And, with that we rolled into the future. And ain't it a son of a bitch to think that we would still need religion to keep the poor from killing the rich," ends the song that begins the album titled *Agnostic Hymns and Stoner Fables.*

Life Challenges

Terror management theory approaches human behavior with two basic assumptions—people know life ends and they want to avoid and distract themselves from that inevitability (Becker 1971). In turn, the bridge between religion and struggle is short, as is the ensuing brief drive to music. Religion and music serve as coping mechanisms. Music provides the cathartic acknowledgment of one's woeful state.

Hank Williams crooned, "Everything's agin me and it's got me down. If I jumped in the river I'd probably drown. No matter how I struggle and strive. I'll never get out of this world alive."[12] Meeting, combating, triumphing over, and occasionally succumbing to life's trials and tribulations is another common theme in Americana music. While Hank Williams is associated with country music, facing or escaping life's challenges is also associated with gospel and the blues (e.g., Jackson 2004; Ward 1998). Howlin' Wolf's plea, "How many more years have I got to let you dog me around? I'd soon rather be dead sleeping six feet in the ground," certainly conveys frustration with life's seemingly insurmountable challenges.[13]

Life's challenges and struggles may or may not incorporate various components, such as romance, family, occupations, avocations, religion/faith, substance abuse, and politics. While religion, region, and agriculture can be addressed by searching for key terms, struggles can only be addressed through contextual review. There are few specific terms that convey struggle and strife in isolation. For example, countless songs across constituent genres reflect alcohol consumption without relaying despair and consternation. Todd Snider's now classic story of fraternity brothers' attempts to secure beer during a Robert Earl Keen concert is upbeat and leaves live audiences laughing. "Found a store with a sign said their beer was coldest. So they sent in Brad 'cause he looked the oldest. He got a case of beer and a candy bar. Walked over to where all the registers are. Laid his fake ID on the countertop. The clerk looked, and turned and looked back up and stopped. And said, 'Boy, I'm not gonna call the cops, but I am keeping this card.' The guys both took it pretty hard."[14]

Slaid Cleaves and Ray Wylie Hubbard's 2004 Americana Music Association-nominated Song of the Year, "Wishbones," presents a very different view from the light-hearted Snider approach. Cleaves conveys depression, suffering, and emptiness associated with alcohol. "Spin the bottle cap, throw a shot back. Everything's gonna be alright. Spin the bottle cap, throw a shot back. Cough and cry, lay down and die."

Roseanne Cash's "Not Many Miles to Go" (2018) illustrates how the hint of alcohol can even be comforting and almost precious. She seemingly sings to her husband, "Time keeps slippin' through the curtain. The Empire State and small-batch bourbon. Now there's not many miles to go, and just one promise left to keep."

Financial distress, manual labor, job loss, and community decimation are also common themes associated with struggle in Americana music. For example, Town Mountain's Jesse Langlais states that their song "Life and Debt" tackles "financial burdens we all shoulder" (pers. interview, August 20, 2021). "Well I went to the man to advance my line. Said 'a hundred

Rod Picott at the Rambling Roots Festival at Tivoli Vrendenburg Utrecht the Netherlands on October 19, 2019. Courtesy Nick Barber.

in cash to get me through hard times.' The banker he looked and shook his head. Said the bank's broke too, ain't got no bread. All the money's in the politicians' hands."[15]

Slaid Cleaves and Rod Picott tackle the deterioration of community in the second verse of "Rust Belt Fields" (2021) "Drove into the ground 'til your factory's cold. Then they tear it all down and the parts get sold. Come the bankers now, picking over the bones. I got three more neighbors now, 'bout to lose their homes." Picott embraces a similar blue-collar point of view laced heavily with coming to acceptance with one's lot in life in "Sheetrock Hanger" (2011), which appears on the same album as his version of "Rust Belt Fields." "I could've gone to school, but I went to work. Guess I'm drinking money, like all the other jerks. I'm pretty sure about this, when I'm gone and dead, if I don't get wings I'll be hanging sheetrock instead."

Such themes have long been prevalent in American Folk music and can be seen in several songs from the Woody Guthrie catalog. "Talking Hard Work" (1961) proffers "I cleaned out 9 barnloads and cranked 31 automobiles, all makes and models. Pulled 3 cars out of mudholes and 4 out of snowdrifts. I dug 5 cisterns of water for some of her friends and neighbors, and run all kinds of errands."

A staggering number of Americana Music Association award-nominated songs address struggles. Greater than 71 percent (sixty-one of eighty-five) do so to some degree. Perhaps more tellingly, 60 percent of *all* nominated Americana Music Association songs (fifty-one of eighty-five) can be said to have struggle as a primary focus.

Perhaps struggle is so pervasive in Americana music because several component constituent genres developed, in part, as a means to deal with life's challenges. Recall the role of religion and gospel on plantations in the rural South, the role of blues in the Mississippi Delta, and the use of bluegrass as a tool to deal with subsistence in poverty-stricken Appalachia. The Thirteenth Amendment to the US Constitution abolished slavery, the conditions forced upon African Americans in the Jim Crow-era South began to improve with the unanimous Supreme Court ruling in *Oliver Brown v. the Board of Education of Topeka, Kansas* (1954), and standards of living in Appalachia are not as dire as during the 1960s, when exposure to photographs of the region partially inspired Lyndon Johnson's War on Poverty.[16] Nevertheless, African Americans consistently face the negative effects of stereotypes (e.g., Peffley and Hurwitz 1997; Peffley, Hurwitz, and Sniderman 1997; Weber, Levine, Huddy, and Federico 2014), and nearly 74 percent of congressional districts in Appalachia (forty-two of fifty-seven) are below the national poverty level (see Fontenot, Semega, and Kollar 2018).[17] Map 2.1 provides an illustration.

Finding race and Appalachia to represent a small portion of nominated songs is surprising. Only eight of the eighty-five songs nominated by the Americana Music Association addressed race directly (9 percent), while a scant four songs reference locations in or adjacent to Appalachia. Notably, these songs include the 2012, 2013, and 2014 Americana Music Association's Songs of the Year and 2021 Song of the Year nominee "A Long Violent History."[18] In the 2013 song "Birmingham," Cary Ann Hearst and Michael Trent, a Charleston, South Carolina-based married couple known as Shovels and Rope, describe struggle and specify "Cumberland" and "Tennessee" in their tale of lovers' travels: "When the road got rough and the wheels all broke. Couldn't take more than we could tow. Making something out of nothing with a scratcher and our hope. Two old guitars like a shovel and a rope."[19]

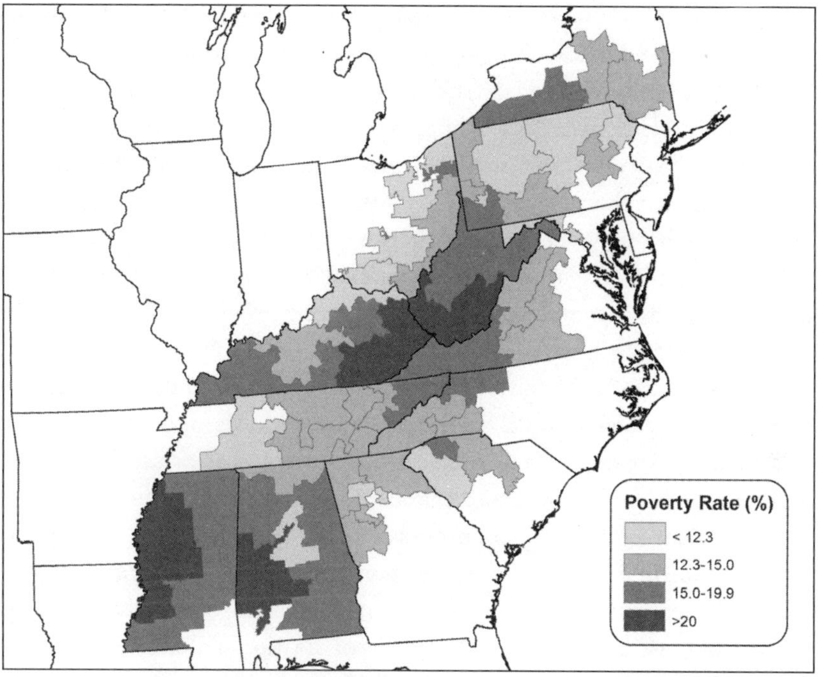

Map. 2.1. Congressional Districts Containing Portions of Appalachia. Courtesy Paul C. Vincent.

Robbie Fulks's 2005 "Georgia Hard" presents a marriage of struggle with the South generally by specifically evoking southern state names and/or agricultural elements associated with specific states/parts of the region. For example, sugarcane production is associated with Florida, Louisiana, and Texas, while bluegrass is associated with Kentucky. Fulks sings, "But there's no Carolina moon over Chicago. No bluegrass growin' out in my backyard. No fields of sugarcane. No soft Virginia rain, but damn if this livin' ain't Georgia Hard."

Politics and Social Awareness

The long history of using music to raise sociopolitical awareness is addressed in the previous chapters. Certainly, music has been an effective tool used by social movements, such as the Student Nonviolent Coordinating

Committee (SNCC), whose efforts routinely included Bob Dylan. The inclusion of Dylan highlighted the group's goals through songs such as "Oxford Town" (1962), in which Dylan tackles the enrollment of the first Black student at the University of Mississippi. "Oxford town around the bend. Came to the door, he couldn't get in. All because of the color of his skin. What do you think about that, my friend?" Inspiration and social justice radiated from civil rights movement artists such as Dylan and Peter, Paul, and Mary, who adapted the African American spiritual "Go Tell It on the Mountain" to represent the movement. "Who's that yonder dressed in black? Let my people go. Must be the hypocrites turnin' back. Let my people go."[20]

The association between folk music particularly and politics has become so closely associated that RB Morris, who is not known for politically laced lyrics, states, "Americana music does not have a 'political' message, but most political songs would fall under that category" (pers. interview, March 5, 2021). While the genre does not necessarily equate to political music, a great deal of music in this space addresses political figures, concepts of nationalism, political divisions, policies, and a general sense of social awareness.

Nearly 11 percent (nine of eighty-three) of titles of albums nominated for Album of the Year by the Americana Music Association contain terms that can be associated with politics and social awareness. Only three of the eighty-five songs nominated for Song of the Year, however, directly used language in the titles reflecting politics or social awareness.[21] This should not be interpreted as Americana Music Association-nominated songs being apolitical in nature.

Nearly one-third of nominated songs (twenty-six of eighty-five) lyrically address politics or social awareness in some way. Approximately 18 percent of nominated songs subtly approach this content, while nearly 13 percent do so overtly. Such overt references include "By Degrees." Several prominent Americana artists joined the song's author, Mike Erelli, on stage at the 2019 Americana Music Awards ceremony in this powerful statement about division, racism, and gun violence.[22] Lori McKenna takes on political division as she sings, "I've seen talking heads shout back and forth across some great divide. Against a map of red and blue. Points of view so cut and dry. But when you look into the mirror what color country do you see? Well, you can learn to live with anything when it happens by degrees." African-born J. S. Ondara, who was nominated as an Emerging Act of the Year in 2019, then tackles racism and hatred: "I've seen the flags at half staff as the nation mourned and moaned. I've seen the stars and bars a'flyin' proud above the state house dome. For the Charleston Nine, we sing I once was blind, but now I see. We can learn to live with anything if it happens by degrees."

Americana music often directly or implicitly challenges political figures. Phil Ochs, who is often remembered as a man described as a journalist by the legendary Bob Dylan, parodies the Johnny Cash classic "Five Feet High and Rising" (1959) in criticizing Richard Nixon.[23] "How high's the Watergate, mama? She said it's one foot high and risin'. How high's the Watergate, papa? He said it's two feet high and risin'. There's a flood around the poker game. There's a bug on the window pane. Gerry Ford must be insane. Oh, my God, it's Mickey Spillane. The tides are risin'. Two feet high and risin'."[24]

James McMurtry's 2008 assessment of George W. Bush is similarly critical. McMurtry is much darker, however. "Another unknown soldier. We've seen it all before. All in the name of Jesus. Behind the razor wire and shackled to the floor. Just keep smiling at the camera. Keep that twinkle in your eye. We don't need to know the answers long as we're safe, hit your marks and say your lines."[25] Will Kimbrough was similarly inspired to address politics during the George W. Bush administration with *Americanitis,* a fully political album.

The Drive-By Truckers are known to tackle sociopolitical issues regularly. "The Perilous Night" (2017) underscores the dangers of misinformation, racism, and Donald Trump: "Dumb, white, and angry with their cup half-filled. Running over people down in Charlottesville. White House fury. It's the killing side he defends." Patterson Hood further doesn't shy away from addressing Trump directly, and he even appeals to the conservatives and evangelicals that lionize Ronald Reagan while supporting Trump: "Ronnie Reagan must be spinning in his grave. Putin's on the rise, Ukraine's under siege. Fascism's knocking and Trump says, 'let them in.' I'd like to tell you there'd be better days. But optimism's running low today. We're off the deep end with a lifeguard that can't swim."

Slaid Cleaves looked to the past to address contemporary politics in his January 2021 YouTube livestream.[26] He begins by describing an unscrupulous landlord's unfair treatment of Portland, Maine, area tenants in the late 1980s, and his writing a song in turn in 1990 when he was part of a band known as the Moxie Men: "He's an upside-down Robin Hood. He gives to the rich and takes from the good. You work for a living the American way, the big men try to take it away. People getting up, taking a stand. Liberty's got a fight on his hands. Too much Liberty in this town. Not enough justice to go around."[27] The landlord Michael Liberty, who was eventually sentenced to four months in prison for illegal campaign contributions, was pardoned by Donald Trump in January 2021.[28] Cleaves clarified that he had not sung this particular song in decades, but he was compelled to include it in the livestream given the timing of the Liberty pardon (pers. interview, February 24, 2021).

While not addressing political figures directly, Son Volt's 2019 *Union* has been characterized as a protest album, and lead Jay Farrar sought inspiration from Woody Guthrie and Mother Jones when recording (Travers 2019). Certainly "Reality Winner," "The Symbol," and "The 99" convey Trump-era dissatisfaction. "While Rome Burns," alternatively, presents a metaphorical accounting of the Trump administration. "Mountains of money. Men dressed up as news. And we fiddle while Rome burns. Like Orwell's doublespeak they're taking their cues. And we fiddle while Rome burns."

John Prine took on symbolic nationalism in 1971 with "Your Flag Decal Won't Get You into Heaven Anymore." In the plain, poetic speak characteristic of the late Prine, a recently deceased man finds himself at the Pearly Gates of Heaven to hear, "But your flag decal won't get you into Heaven anymore. We're already over-crowded from your dirty little war. Now Jesus don't like killin' no matter what the reason for. And your flag decal won't get you into Heaven anymore."

Shovels and Rope takes an especially empathetic perspective on immigration. In "C'mon, Utah," Cary Ann Hearst and Michael Trent sing, "I was thirsty, I was lost. I was hanging from a cross. I was dying to make it back to Colorado. Bones in the saddle, I was weary from the battle. The path was much too difficult to follow. Well, come on Utah. Get me over that hill. We got ten more miles, oh now, turn that dial. We're never coming back again. Well, come on Utah. Raise me over that ledge. I wanna see my son and carry my gun like a real American."[29] Hearst and Trent further make immigration and their position on the United States' southern boarder wall proposal associated with Donald Trump clear in a children's book with the same name as the song. The book focuses on the fictional aftermath of the wall by providing an inspirational community-based story.[30]

In the previously addressed "Sheetrock Hanger" (2021), Rod Picott seemingly takes a more ambivalent approach to the impact of immigration.

"Things ain't the same here since the Mexicans came here. I'm not saying they're to blame. Twenty years now the money still ain't changed." This contemplation, which can also be seen in "Rust Belt Fields," can be interpreted from a blue-collar perspective that leans to the political left, or as a more nuanced perspective through lyrics such as "But they figured it out and sent the elbow grease down to Mexico and off to the Chinese. And I learned a little something 'bout the way things are. No one remembers your name just for working hard."[31]

While contemporary country music has been criticized for its seeming failure to include LGBTQ+ artists and related lyrics, Americana has often embraced the community. Brandi Carlile, a successful, openly gay Americana artist, remarked during her 2019 Grammy acceptance speech, "Americana music is an island of misfit toys and I'm such a misfit." Carlile, a member of The Highwomen, sings lead on "If She Ever Leaves Me," a 2019 lesbian love song written by Jason Isbell, Amanda Shires, and Chris Tompkins. Further, the character at the center of Hayes Carll's (2005) "Good Friends" expresses clear acceptance of a gay friend, "And Mikey took some time, and found out he was gay. I didn't have the heart to tell him that we all knew anyway."

These were not the first songs to address the LGBTQ+ community in Americana, however. Rodney Crowell addresses the relationship between twin brothers, one gay with AIDS and one straight, in 2001's "Wandering Boy." "I used to cast my judgments like a net. All those California gay boys deserve what they get. Little did I know there would come a day when my words would come back screaming like a debt I have to pay. Lean on me. I'll be strong. We're almost free. It won't be long. Wandering boy."

While gun violence, poverty, diversity, and politics as portrayed in Americana music are generally important, race is clearly a seminal focus of this research. Todd Snider tackles racism, crime, and stereotypes head-on in "The Devil You Know" (2006). "Helicopters over the house again. We got the projects two or three blocks from here. They pull these kids over for driving-while-African. And the ones with the warrants all run in fear . . . This poor kid probably never had a chance to give a fuck. He wouldn't know good luck from a debutante. He's got to find a way to be Steve McNair or Young Buck. Or he's just tough luck looking for a prison to haunt."

Tim O'Brien addresses race in different ways by memorializing the late civil rights activist and congressman John Lewis and by presenting a fic-

Tim O'Brien at the Rocky Mountain Folks Festival in Lyons, Colorado, on August 18, 2008. Courtesy Nick Barber.

tional account of a meeting between two of Thomas Jefferson's children in a 2021 album. In "When You Pray (Move Your Feet)" O'Brien sings, "When a hard rain blows and the clouds rain down, move your feet and make a joyful sound. The Lord is listening. He's watching too. He'll keep you safe and he'll push you through. John Lewis gone his words ring on, clap your hands and help me sing this song." Alternatively, O'Brien encourages listeners to think about the Jefferson family and, in turn, other interracial families in early America through a spoken introduction in "Can You See Me, Sister?" "Some years after the death of his wife, Thomas Jefferson took his slave, Sally Hemings as his consort. She had several children by Jefferson, and all of those that survived were eventually granted their freedom. One of the younger sons, Madison, corresponded with his older, light-skinned sister, Harriet, who had married and passed into white Washington society. At some point, she stopped returning his letters. This song imagines a chance encounter between the two on the street somewhere."

Tyler Childers takes an entirely different tack in addressing race by putting himself, a young, white, southern Appalachian man, in the same position as Breonna Taylor, a young African American woman who was killed by police in her Louisville home, in "A Long Violent History." In the 2021 Americana Music Association-nominated Song of the Year, Childers sings, "Now, what would you get if you heard my opinion. Conjecturin' on matters that I ain't never dreamed. In all my born days as a white boy from Hickman, based on the way the world's been to me? It's called me belligerent, it's took me for ignorant. But, it ain't never once made me scared just to be. Could you imagine just constantly worryin'. Kickin' and fightin' just beggin' to breathe."

Examples of political commentary—and commentary related specifically to race—has historically been an inherent thread of American folk music. Roy (2010) states that while European folk music is often associated with nationalistic sentiments, that is not the case in the United States, where folk music has become intrinsically linked to the downtrodden, racial minorities, and the political left. Therefore, we must consider throughout this analysis of Americana music that all music in this space can ultimately be seen as political even if the content cannot be characterized as such.

While politics, social awareness, struggle, religion, agriculture, and region are all dominant themes in Americana music, the content analysis used here illustrates that none of these substantive foci are crucial in defining Americana music. Eleven of the songs nominated for Song of the Year by the Americana Music Association fail to include one of these themes. To that end, I end this section with the knowledge that Americana music likely includes one of these foci, but it doesn't have to.

Narrative

A consistent theme throughout the majority of the interviews elucidated in the following chapter is the power of narrative. Americana artists embrace their role as storytellers. RB Morris eloquently describes this process as so powerful that its impact across generations is incalculable: "It ebbs and surges as to what degree and in how many ways it reaches audiences, but audiences are always open and available to its influence" (pers. interview, March 5, 2021). His description of narrative power speaks directly to narrative transportation theory.

Narratives don't just vary in terms of content. The period of time they convey in songs can be as brief as a moment, as described in the 2002-nominated humorous bluegrass song "She's Looking at Me," performed by Jim Lauderdale, and Ralph Stanley and the Clinch Mountain Boys, or as long as the lifetime that lovers spend together, as conveyed in Robert Ellis's 2014 Americana Music Association-nominated Best Song, "The Light from the Chemical Plant."[32]

Sixty of the eighty-five songs (70.59 percent) nominated for Song of the Year by the Americana Music Association utilize narrative. While this staggering volume of nominated music's use of narrative suggests that narrative is a critical element of Americana music, the remaining twenty-two songs that do not incorporate narrative illustrate that its use is not absolutely necessary to achieving Americana classification.

Moreover, music journalist and research editor for *Rolling Stone* Jonathon Bernstein acknowledges that Americana music does an exceptionally good job with storytelling and conveying authenticity (pers. interview, March 17, 2021). Bernstein warns, however, that separate musical genres, such as rap, which is also rooted in the United States, also often rely on narrative.

Singer-Songwriters

In some ways I have seemingly done little more than reiterate utilizing constituent genres of Americana music to define the format at this point. Nevertheless, the focus on titles and content has provided a broader view of the messages artists in this space send and the stories they tell. Further the lyrics are not created in a vacuum. The authenticity conveyed in Americana lyrics, regardless of content and across constituent genres, is crucial and leads to the remaining unexplored component of Americana music—songwriting.

Hayes Carll and Darrell Scott's "For the Sake of the Song" does more than identify constituent genres (e.g., folk, rock, country, delta blues). As noted at the onset of this chapter, that particular song also conjures images of the artists themselves. The artists, like the harmonicas used in folk, the mandolins and banjos used in bluegrass, and the guitars used across constituent genres, are pivotal to understanding the music. More specifically, one needs to look beyond the lyrics to seeing whether the person singing the lead is also a songwriter. In fact, Rod Picott and Jamie Anderson each identify as a songwriter first and an Americana musician second (Picott pers. interview, April 12, 2021; Anderson pers. interview, June 7, 2021).

Likewise, Colin Gilmore indirectly provides a link between songwriting, personal resonance via narrative transport, and the common man, as addressed in the introduction of this book (pers. interview, December 21, 2021): "I think Americana has a sense of humility and storytelling that lends itself to political messaging . . . messages of value, and trying to see things through people's eyes that have been through rough times. I feel like now so many Americana musicians are not living these super rough lifestyles, but they're still trying to see things through the eyes of people that are or who have. . . . There is that sentiment of wanting to lift people from the bottom up."

Prior to moving forward with this discussion, pointing out that Americana artists often play cover songs is necessary. Indeed, Aengus Finnan explains that the progression of one's career on stage often begins by including covers and transitions to performing one's own material and including covers written by friends (pers. interview, May 18, 2021). Certainly, some covers are as identifiable as the original, and sometimes even more so. Jerry Jeff Walker embraced Ray Wylie Hubbard's "Up Against the Wall Redneck Mother" (1973) and Rusty Wier's "Don't It Make You Want to Dance" (1975). Townes Van Zandt covered the Rolling Stones' "Dead Flowers."[33] RB Morris has sung "The Late John Garfield Blues" both with writer John Prine and solo.[34] Todd Snider even recorded a tribute album to Walker, and several Americana artists contributed to 2011's *This One's for Him: A Tribute to Guy Clark,* which was nominated for Album of the Year by the Americana Music Association in 2012, four years before Clark's passing.[35]

The list of covers is limitless, but what is missing from simply stating that these artists employ songs written by others is that they are still writers themselves. Walker wrote a number of songs over the course of decades, including "Mr. Bojangles" (1968). Townes Van Zandt wrote "Pancho and Lefty" (1972). Prine covered Morris's "That's How Every Empire Falls" (2016). Further, Snider has a long-standing career as a songwriter involving

Todd Snider and John Prine at the Ryman Auditorium on April 20, 2019. Courtesy Stacie Huckeba.

much more than the aforementioned "In the Beginning," "Beer Run," and "The Devil You Know." He penned "Alright Guy" (1994), "Late Last Night" (1996), and "Play a Train Song" (2004), which have been covered by other artists. Robert Earl Keen recorded "Play a Train Song," while Cross Canadian Ragweed covered the others. Moreover, Cody Canada reports continuing to cover "Betty Was Black (and Willie Was White)" after the dissolution of Cross Canadian Ragweed (pers. interview, March 29, 2021). He credits Snider and Will Kimbrough for the song, which Snider recorded in 2000 but Kimbrough wrote and first recorded with the Bis-Quits in 1993.[36] Keen and Canada are also accomplished songwriters.[37]

While not all songs nominated for awards by the Americana Music Association were written by the performers, all of the nominated artists can be characterized as singer-songwriters. This also applies to many of the individuals (e.g., Will Kimbrough, Buddy Miller, Tim O'Brien, Darrell Scott) nominated for instrumental awards. Simply put, Americana artists write. Therefore, in addition to Americana music existing within or across bluegrass, blues, country, cowpunk, folk, gospel, jazz, rock and roll, rockabilly, and southern rock, it is also played, in part, by someone best characterized as a singer-songwriter.

Summary

This chapter addresses the dominant constituent genres in the Americana format before delving deeply into lyrical content. Playing within or across the component constituent genres is likely necessary to achieve classification as Americana, but it is not sufficient. Further, several dominant themes can be seen across the music—agriculture, region, religion, struggle, politics, and social awareness. None of these themes is required, however. Narrative writing is also characteristic of this format, but it is similarly not required.

Singer-songwriters occupy this space. Bernstein suggests this type of artist is pivotal to the authenticity conveyed by the medium (pers. interview, March 17, 2021). Indeed, this authenticity is inherent in the thematic elements of Americana music. The presence of a singer-songwriter is necessary in the genre. The writing is key and cements the constituent genre into a collective. More specifically, taken together, constituent genres classification and the presence of a singer-songwriter are necessary and sufficient to label music as Americana, and as concisely noted by Darrell Scott in "Down to the River" (2016), "And we won't give a damn if it's rock, folk, country, or blues."

›››››› 3 ‹‹‹‹‹‹

THE ARTISTS

Cody Jinks's 2017 song title "Raisin' Hell with the Hippies and the Cowboys" and Guy Clark's "Lone Star Hotel" (1981) potentially reinforce commonly held stereotypes associated with Americana artists. Clark sings, "So here's to you west Texas, you old rodeo queen. How I miss your beer joints and shuffle board machines. Here's to you west Texas, how I miss the smell of greasy enchiladas and the old Lone Star Hotel." Clark's role in Americana culture deserves greater attention beyond "Lone Star Hotel" or any single song, however.

"Back when down on my luck kept me up for days. You were there with the right word to help me crawl out of the maze," Rodney Crowell writes of Guy Clark in the 2017 Americana Music Association's Song of the Year.[1] Indeed, many Americana artists see Clark as having the right words. When asked about his own move to Nashville, Rod Picott says, "Once I arrived in Nashville I realized that my peers weren't the cashier at the vegan grocery but John Prine, Lucinda Williams, and Guy Clark. It was a big smack upside the head, but I took it on. I said to myself, 'Okay the cones have been moved now. This is how good you have to write'" (pers. interview, July 7, 2021). This sentiment not only applies to Clark's genius, but also speaks to the culture of Americana. More specifically, Clark was a Texan that became pivotal to aspiring songwriters in Nashville.[2]

As illustrated in the preceding chapters, Americana's roots and reach are diverse, but the Americana ethos is often centered in Texas and Tennessee. This chapter considers the artists, their thoughts about their music, and their thoughts about the relationship between the Americana culture and politics/race/social awareness. In order to understand artist motivations,

John Paul White and Rodney Crowell, taken on February 25, 2017 in Cayamo, Gulf of Mexico, aboard the *Norwegian Jade*. Courtesy Michelle Stancil.

creative processes, and their perceptions of the culture, personal interviews were conducted between February and August of 2021.[3]

Sampling Approach

Americana charts and Americana Music Association award nominations provided a starting point for sample collection. This approach, however, neglects notable artists within specific constituent genres and narrows the time frame of released music. In order to somewhat ameliorate these concerns, I contacted managers, festival organizers, publicists, and even the artists themselves and asked for recommendations of other artists in this space. Thus, artist selection was not random, and a snowball sampling approach was employed. One-third (33.33 percent) of contacted artists participated. The response rate among male artists was considerably higher (48.57 percent) than the response rate among female artists (17.65 percent).

Notably, the twenty-three artists included in this study represent varied career stages, constituent genres, and differing geographic ties. Further, they are an accomplished group netting thirty-five Grammy nominations, eight Grammy wins, thirty-three Americana Music Association award nominations, and ten Americana Music Association award wins. Table 3.1 illustrates those artists included in this research and notes wins and nominations for both Americana Music Association awards and Recording Academy Grammys.

Contributing artists have recorded nearly three hundred combined albums across constituent genres over more than five decades. I must note, however, that, despite the accolades and volume of work, the dominance of heterosexual white men addressed in chapter 1 is reflected in the artists interviewed in this volume.[4] Seventeen of these twenty-three artists identify as such. One heterosexual African American man (Reggie Harris) participated in the interviews, while four heterosexual white women and one heterosexual Korean woman (BettySoo) participated. There is little variation in sexual orientation. One contributing female artist, Jamie Anderson, identifies as lesbian, however.

While there is little variation in sexual orientation, gender, and race, the sample age range varies from twenty-seven to seventy-two at the time interviewed. Moreover, the sample includes three international artists (Aengus Finnan, Anana Kaye, and Irakli Gabriel), one American living abroad (Jamie Anderson), and one Jewish artist (Bernice Lewis). Notably, only ten of the artists interviewed are currently based in Texas or Tennessee, and sampled artists were raised in a variety of settings with parents representing a number of professions, such as psychologist, educator, musician, and, in the case of Will Kimbrough, a US district attorney.[5]

Introspection and awareness of ambiguity can be used to broadly define this group relating to attitudes toward politically laced and/or socially aware lyrics. Some prefer subtlety, while others hit political messaging head-on. For example, Irakli Gabriel says, "you can do a lot with metaphor," while Patterson Hood says of the Drive-By Truckers, "I've always considered us political . . . to the point that when there was this public outcry we were all kind of taken aback. It was like, have you been listening?" (Gabriel pers. in-

Table 3.1. Sampled Artists

Artist/s (Act)	*Americana Music Association Awards Nominations*	*Americana Music Association Awards Wins*	*Grammy Nominations*	*Grammy Wins*
Jamie Anderson	0	0	0	0
BettySoo	0	0	0	0
Cody Canada	0	0	0	0
Slaid Cleaves	2	0	0	0
Rodney Crowell[EH,CA]	11	5	16	2
Kristen Englenz	0	0	0	0
Aengus Finnan	0	0	0	0
Robbie Fulks	0	0	2	0
Eliza Gilkyson	0	0	2	0
Colin Gilmore	0	0	0	0
Reggie Harris	0	0	0	0
Patterson Hood (Drive-By Truckers)	6	1	0	0
Anana Kaye & Irakli Gabriel (Anana Kaye)	0	0	0	0
Will Kimbrough	4	1	0	0
Jessie Langlais (Town Mountain)	0	0	0	0
Bernice Lewis	0	0	0	0
RB Morris	0	0	0	0
Tim O'Brien[CA]	1	0	6	2
Rod Picott	0	0	0	0
Joel Rafael	0	0	0	0
Darrell Scott[BOJ,CA]	4	2	4	0
Todd Snider (Solo/ Hard Working Americans)	2	0	0	0
John Paul White[RC] (The Civil Wars)	3	2	5	4

[EH] Rodney Crowell has been nominated for Americana Music Awards as a solo artist and for work with Emmylou Harris.

[CA] Three contributing artists are included on the 2012 Guy Clark tribute album, which won album of the year. The tribute album nomination/win is not included in the table above.

[BOJ] Nominations include Robert Plant's Band of Joy.

[RC] One nomination and win in collaboration with Rodney Crowell.

terview, February 13, 2021; Hood pers. interview, February 19, 2021). Certainly, much of the Drive-By Truckers repertoire had been politically laced far earlier than the 2020 release of *The Unraveling,* which Hood sees as a point at which those with only a cursory understanding of the band began to realize the subject matter and inspiration behind their music. Hood speculates that the more contemporary nature of *The Unraveling* gave the album a political urgency (pers. interview, February 19, 2021).

Alternatively, Anana Kaye and Irakli Gabriel see timelessness as a powerful musical device. Kaye points to Bob Dylan's "The Times They Are A-Changin'" (1963) as an example of thoughtful music that applies across generations (pers. interview, February 13, 2021). The duo and the late David Olney appear to be tackling Trump-era politics in "The Last Days of Rome" on their 2021 *Whispers and Sighs* album. The lyrics, however, like Dylan's 1964 classic, are designed to elicit contemplation rather than a stagnant historical point. Written in 2018, two years before Donald Trump used the Bible as a prop in the wake of peaceful protests outside of St. John's Episcopal Church in Washington, DC, igniting a firestorm of criticism from the Episcopal Church and greater Christian community, "The Last Days of Rome" sounds as if Olney, Kaye, and Gabriel were channeling the event.[6] "Wrapped in a flag, Holy Book in his hand. The leader stands on a pedestal."[7]

Notably, some artists, such as BettySoo, Colin Gilmore, and John Paul White, do not tackle partisan politics directly in music, but praise others that do. BettySoo points to Ray Wylie Hubbard and Hayes Carll as examples of articulate, socially aware artists, while Gilmore references Steve Earle (BettySoo pers. interview, September 21, 2021; Gilmore pers. interview, December 21, 2021). White contends, "I don't consider myself a political artist, but I consider everything on the table.... I probably could never be Patterson or Mike Cooley or Jason Isbell. I don't have the same kind of passion that they do. Sometimes I'm ashamed of that. I feel there's a guilt-level that happens with me that I'm not more overt... but at the end of the day I know I'm trying to do my part and I'm raising my children to do that" (pers. interview, May 10, 2021).

This chapter advances by considering artists' lyrical intent as well as their thoughts of the genre and constituent genres. I begin by considering artists' reflections of this musical space and their individual roles in it specifically before moving into the consideration of politics, race, and social awareness. I then compare the thoughts of the female and African American artists to those of the heterosexual white men to find a great deal of homogeneity in opinion related to race and social awareness. Importantly, while this research is principally concerned with race, diversity more broadly is an important consideration. Extant research points to the linkage of various aspects of diversity into a multicultural perspective (e.g., ethnicity, gender, race, sexual orientation) (e.g., Goldberg 1994). Thus, this chapter concludes by discussing two notable themes in contributing interviews—a desire for inclusivity broadly and the understanding of ambiguity in terms of message and audience.

Resistance to Labeling

The notion of labeling is often uncomfortable, yet categorizing is a key psychological resource. In order to make sense of the world, humans engage in social categorization by placing others into groups (e.g., gender, race, age, nationality). Allport (1954, 42) states in his seminal study of social interaction that the human mind simply can't work without the categorization process, "Orderly living depends upon it."

I came to understand that, while this cognitive framework is necessary for understanding stereotyping, categorization for artists can come with a bitter taste. Pivotal to this research is understanding what Americana music is and who Americana artists are. The preceding chapters suggest that Americana is as much about the culture as it is about the sounds. Perhaps Rod Picott addressed this best by noting, "there's no one sound" (pers. interview, June 3, 2021). Nevertheless, understanding the culture necessitates understanding the artists and their intent. I asked each artist his or her preferred label, and there was either notable hesitancy or an insistence on clarification even for those artists that closely identify with a particular genre. I was typically given an explanation based in message rather than musicality by those that identified with a particular constituent genre, and hesitant artists insisted on blurring the lines between musical styles and categories.

It is this blurring that, for some, is the draw of Americana. Tim O'Brien, who has earned six Grammy nominations and two wins (one for Best Bluegrass Album and one for Best Traditional Folk Album) jokes that those artists who occupied early Americana charts were referred to by the Nashville music industry establishment as "has-beens and never-weres."[8] "I guess I was a never-was," O'Brien reasoned (pers. interview, February 24, 2021). He further addresses the difficulty in pinpointing his brand of music by noting that some bluegrass purists do not warm to his work, and he similarly does not fit purely into old-time music, which is also associated with folk. O'Brien indicates that Hot Rize, the bluegrass band on which he initially established his national/international reputation, was not comprised of members identifying as southern Appalachian and was heavily influenced by folk and popular music of the late 1960s and early 1970s. "In bluegrass we were always renegades. We couldn't really fit in with the good ole boys in the way someone from Georgia or Tennessee could. . . . [The music,] our accents, the way in which we carried ourselves was different" (pers. interview, February 24, 2021).

BettySoo, Colin Gilmore, Reggie Harris, RB Morris, and Jesse Langlais of Town Mountain further underscore this point. Morris refers to Americana as a "broad tent" (pers. interview, March 5, 2021). When asked if he identifies as an Americana artist, Morris says "yes and no" while acquiescing that there likely is not a better label for him. Gilmore also identifies as an Americana artist, but is quick to note that his musical influences are varied, and he describes his music as roots-based rock and roll and roots-based folk. "I go into music with a roots-based perspective, but sometimes something more rock and roll comes out" (pers. interview, December 21, 2021). Similarly, Langlais notes that the "folk musics" that encompass the space offer fluidity and room to grow for artists (pers. interview, August 20, 2021).

Harris recognizes this room for growth as well, stating that while his roots are in folk and gospel, he feels he has the ability to "stretch" and try new styles (pers. interview, August 24, 2021). BettySoo also points to the flexibility in Americana music allowing for an authenticity in message. She reports that "most folks who are in my slice of the music world have traded away any ambitions for fame—and really a lasting legacy—for some level of 'authentic' pursuit of art or craft of the issues and themes we find interesting, of the stories we find compelling" (pers. interview, September 21, 2021).

While Langlais is quick to note that Town Mountain's roots are firmly in bluegrass, the band has stretched beyond the traditional five-piece bluegrass band (banjo, mandolin, fiddle, guitar, and bass) to a much bigger sound that even includes drums. Like O'Brien, Langlais wonders if the bluegrass purists

Town Mountain at the Salvage Station in Asheville, North Carolina, July 31, 2021. Photo courtesy John Zara.

remain fans of Town Mountain, but happily recognizes the band's ability to cultivate loyalty among existing fans while broadening their fan base (pers. interview, August 20, 2021).

Saviano's (2016) biography of Guy Clark discusses the *Gavin Report* as well as the establishment of the Americana charts, which sought to embrace this ambiguity in roots music. Moreover, the foundation of the Americana charts emphasized artists that could be characterized as songwriters (although playing covers and standards has always been part of this musical space), received a great deal of critical praise, and toured with loyal fan bases. From the onset, Americana as a radio format, in turn, celebrated those artists for which commercial radio was simply uninterested. Indeed, the 1992 issue of the *Gavin Report* was titled, "Gavin Celebrates American Music: The Singer/Songwriter Issue," and featured four cover photos of Americana artists—John Prine, James McMurtry, John Trudell, and Kevin Welch.[9] While not presented in photographs, the cover also noted an additional four artists, two of whom are often recognized as Americana artists—Rosie Flores and Jim Lauderdale.[10] The inclusion of Trudell, a Native American, and Flores, a Latina, is notable.

Todd Snider at the Ryman Auditorium in Nashville, Tennessee, on October 17, 2016. Courtesy James Martin.

While genre is somewhat of a focal point of this research, musicians may look to other methods of categorization. Musical production and one's sense of touring may color artists' conceptions of labeling. For instance, Bernice Lewis wonders how much of what we conceptualize as folk and Americana is characterized by an acoustic delivery (pers. interview, March 26, 2021). Further, Will Kimbrough notes that the level of production may or may not influence one's notion of Americana (pers. interview, March 4, 2021). He further notes that if something he does has a lot of electric guitar and drums he calls it Americana, otherwise he calls it folk—but "Primarily, I'm a songwriter." Notably, the acts of writing and touring are intrinsically linked in many artists' self-conceptions. Todd Snider, characterizing himself as a troubadour, provides an apt illustration of this relationship (pers. interview, May 21, 2021).

Politics and Social Awareness

While the reaction to musical labeling could be seen as collectively tepid by contributing artists, one could not collectively label this group as embracing or rejecting partisan political themes. Indeed, a willingness to embrace political positioning can be seen by some of those artists included, while others cautiously and perhaps begrudgingly traipse into political debate. Others still prefer to insinuate rather than articulate issues that could be seen as political.

Political scientists often conflate partisan politics and social awareness. This is for good reason, as the allocation of need and/or distribution of resources depends on a given individual's sense of need and/or understanding of how to best distribute resources. This type of evaluation is at the crux of David Easton's seminal *A Framework for Political Analysis.* Easton (1965) sees political life as dependent on the social and political environment. Nevertheless, partisan politics, or what Americans may term as "red and blue," is an oversimplification of societal values. Several of the contributing artists found social awareness and partisan politics to be quite distinct. For example, when asked about whether he considers his music political, Darrell Scott said, "I hardly even know what political means anymore." He says he thinks of himself as "fighting for the looked-over people" (pers. interview, April 21, 2021).

Colin Gilmore takes an honest and practical approach to overtly political themes. He states that, "I've never been great at getting a political message across so I don't really go for that. And, I've seen it done right before. I'm the kind of guy that if I go that route, I want to do it well" (pers. interview, December 21, 2021). Nevertheless, his response to social awareness in his music speaks as much to the broader Americana culture as to himself. "There's not a lot of direct political messages or sentiment in my music. . . . When I write, I try to come from that place of humility and general fascination at the world. . . . A lot of like-minded people are in this [musical space] so it can be that way," Gilmore says of the potential for audiences less familiar with his work—but with general familiarity of Americana—to perceive most music in this space to be politically laced or twinged with social awareness.

At the root of this research is the notion that music can be a tool that can both impact and reflect attitudes. The power of folk music specifically was evident in the work of the Highlander Folk School, which utilized music directors to train civil rights activists and icons such as Rosa Parks and John Lewis and whose efforts led to the founding of the Student Nonviolent Coordinating Committee (SNCC).[11] Nevertheless, music's current place in the broad political environment is questionable. RB Morris summarizes this notion by suggesting that commercialization potentially deserves some blame. "I think American music has been one of the great ambassadors for democracy and freedom in general around the world. But I think that influence has greatly diminished in the last generation or so. There are many factors involved in this, but basically as the music industry became more about money, sponsorship, other connected lines of business and branding, and categorizing, it became less influential politically and culturally. Or, to say, its cultural influence became less political" (pers. interview, March 5, 2021).

Activism and Education

Several of the artists contributing to this study have taken active roles in advancing social causes and/or utilizing their talents and performances to educate. In fact, Bernice Lewis, who occasionally incorporates her Jewish heritage into her work, formally teaches songwriting and often presents "History Alive," a program reflective of her own family's struggles to escape Nazi Germany in the 1940s (pers. interview, March 26, 2021). Nevertheless, Lewis is clear that she has not tried to sustain a living as a holocaust educator, and rarely incorporates related songs when performing for a generic audience. "It's a very tricky topic. So dark."

Nevertheless, Lewis specifically points to an experience teaching consecutive eighth grade English classes in illustrating the power of music to impart history and cultural diversity. "I opened my mouth and started to talk about how my father was thirteen years old and living on the streets of Paris while it was occupied by Nazi soldiers, and these thirteen-year-olds sat up in their seats" (pers. interview, March 26, 2021). At that point, Lewis says, she pulled out her guitar, "and when you have a guitar they think you're cool."

Will Kimbrough at a Songwriting With Soldiers retreat in August 2021. Courtesy Ed Rode.

Like Lewis, Will Kimbrough also uses music to educate. As a songwriter for Songwriting With Soldiers, he feels the songs he cowrites with the extended military community in the program can increase social awareness of the challenges faced by them (pers. interview, March 4, 2021).[12] Of working with soldiers, Kimbrough says, "We're bearing witness. . . . We're not there to give our opinion in any way, shape, or form. We're just listening for the song and the story."

Reggie Harris similarly sees education as being a key facet of his profession. Harris, whose career has spanned decades (as a solo artist and as half of Reggie and Kim) and includes training with the Highlander Folk School

Reggie Harris and Pete Seeger at the Rosendale Recreation Center in Rosendale, New York, on November 3, 2013. Courtesy Russell Cusick.

as well as professional and friendly relationships with musical icons in civil rights such as Pete Seeger and Guy and Candy Carawan, travels extensively across the United States and Canada to educate about past injustices and discuss efforts to promote racial/ethnic inclusivity and community building. "The sixties weren't the first time that people of different backgrounds worked together for justice. And that has been one of the main themes of my work for the entirety of my career," Harris says of the need to understand multiculturalism in ameliorating the ills of slavery and segregation (pers. interview, August 24, 2021).

While Joel Rafael does not offer educational series, like Harris, activism has impacted his life and career. Rafael speaks of his father's running for a school board position in suburban Los Angeles to prevent the ascension of John Birch Society candidates, his organization of a school bus walk-off complete with alerting local newspapers in response to what the students perceived as unfair treatment by the bus driver, and his successfully evasion of the Vietnam War draft by relocating to the Oregon wilderness and repeatedly changing addresses with the draft board (pers. interview, April 2, 2021).[13] He reports seeing an important distinction between the broader Americana format and folk music, with the latter being intrinsically tied to addressing events occurring in one's community: "The songs of the sixties... many of those that Bob Dylan wrote in the early days, were very much just about the issues and what was going on." Rafael sees what is commonly referred to as folk in recent decades as lacking that focus on the issues.

Like Dylan, Rafael also wrote about the 1955 lynching of Emmett Till, a fourteen-year-old African American boy in Money, Mississippi. Dylan's account presents the brutal slaying in stark terms. "Then they rolled his body down a gulf amidst a bloody red rain. And they threw him in the waters wide to cease his screaming pain. The reason they killed him there, and I'm sure it ain't no lie, was just for the fun of killin' him and to watch him slowly die."[14] Rafael takes a different tack in 2019's "Glory Bound" by emphasizing the resultant positive impact that Till's death had on the civil rights movement. In reference to Money and Till's legacy, Rafael sings, "You can lay your money down, I am glory bound."

Robbie Fulks, who is not known for consistent and/or overtly partisan performances, also presented audiences with a moment for activism during the 2020 presidential campaign. Fulks admits that during the Biden-Trump contest he "got to a point with it where [I] had just never gotten during presidential contests before. I just couldn't shut my mouth any more for some reason... I felt I had to contribute in some way to what seemed to be potentially disastrous" (pers. interview, April 19, 2021). In response, Fulks utilized a virtual performance to support Democratic candidate Joseph Biden by sending proceeds to the Democratic National Committee. If individual audience members did not want to support Biden and/or the Democratic Party, however, Fulks made clear during the event that he and fellow organizers would "pocket" the funds rather than utilizing them to support Biden. Fulks reports that Trump supporters' reactions varied from "we'll never buy your records again" to "we don't support what you did, but we'll still support you."

Contemplation, Moderation, and Subtlety

Robbie Fulks's decision to fundraise for the 2020 Democratic presidential candidate should not be confused with a desire to transition into an overtly partisan performer. Indeed, Fulks sees danger in partisan polarization, noting that he sees the extreme left as "unrealistic" and the extreme right as "dangerous." He further endeavors "not to signal the usual lines of division" when tackling issues (pers. interview, April 19, 2021). This desire to reason through contemporary partisan divisions is characteristic of several included artists.

Colin Gilmore, who avoids overt political messaging, speaks to concerns about political tribalism and the danger in signaling divides in a manner reminiscent of social identity theory. Tajfel and Turner's (1979) classic work is rooted in in-groups and out-groups and implies that how one sees the world and others is dependent on how one perceives themself. More specifically, individuals categorize those around them based on how they see themselves and whether they categorize others in a relatable fashion (in-groups) or sense distinctions between themselves and others (out-groups). This categorization process may lead to "in-group favoritism" (e.g., Brewer 1979) and "out-group derogation" (e.g., Hinkle and Brown 1990). Moreover, research has specifically linked partisanship to social identity (e.g., Huddy, Mason, and Aaroe 2015) and additional scholarship states that "Republicans are more reliant than are Democrats on their social identities for constructing strong partisan attachments" (Mason and Wronski 2018, 274).

Gilmore didn't assign political partisanship to his observation about growing polarization in American politics. Rather, he noted that while he chooses not to engage in directly political performances, the audience's perception of the musical space may nevertheless signal those divides: "It's a modern thing in politics to really want to find your tribe and be leery of the other side. . . . People want to draw really sharp lines. It's necessary sometimes, but it can be detrimental. . . . It makes it difficult to learn from the people you disagree with" (pers. interview, December 21, 2021). Gilmore further indicates that he's seen performers address politics and social awareness in a way that communicates "human morality" rather than triggering division and fear: "I admire the people that do it gracefully. . . . But, if nothing else, I don't want to add to people having rotten attitudes toward each other because of my music."

Tim O'Brien explains that his two oldest siblings had a profound impact on him before noting that there was a cultural shift with his older sister Mollie and him (pers. interview, February 24, 2021). "Politics is sort of in the background for me all along. . . . My two oldest brothers were in the military. The oldest brother went to Vietnam and died there. He was a ninety-day wonder lieutenant in the marines. . . . My surviving brother went to the Naval Academy. . . . He got his retirement from the navy."

Mollie and Tim O'Brien gravitated toward musicians and actors who embraced more leftist and progressive politics. Nevertheless, O'Brien emphasizes, "In my world politics isn't so black and white because my brother died in Vietnam and I honor both my brothers serving in the military. . . . I can't ignore the opposing view because I feel like it's part of me." While O'Brien identifies as somewhat left-leaning and recognizes the role politics plays in his art, he endeavors to take alternative views into consideration and chooses to support Get Out the Vote (GOTV) efforts rather than support an individual candidate. "I've often made in recent election years, make the announcement sometimes at the end of the show, 'Just reminding you to get out and vote, to research, and to read widely. Choose your candidates based on some real research, not just what you see on Facebook.'"

O'Brien's 2021 album *He Walked On* features artwork reflective of this contemplation. The album title and title track are obvious references to civil rights icon John Lewis, but the watercolor painting features a faceless white man. "The guy is a 'sorta me,' walking through the world trying to make sense, learn, enjoy, find the real thing, etc. . . . I did wonder if [the hat] could be a MAGA hat and thought, that's a good thing to come up and leave unanswered. And the CD is conceptually about America, so the colors suggest that. Making those things was really fun—I just didn't look up for a couple weeks. I worked just long enough on the human form to show it walking away to the left!" (pers. interview, July 19, 2021).

Will Kimbrough also points to the value of moderation. Like O'Brien, Kimbrough identifies as leaning liberal and does not hide his views from audiences, but eschews the notion of diving too deeply into partisan politics. Kimbrough describes the recent dissolution of a band he fronted following the polarization of two band members. "They just kind of removed themselves from anyone that didn't have their political beliefs, which I would say are pretty far to the right, and they became pretty belligerent about it online. . . . I'm not going to fire a member of the band because of their political beliefs unless they do something that actually hurts people" (pers. interview, March 4, 2021).

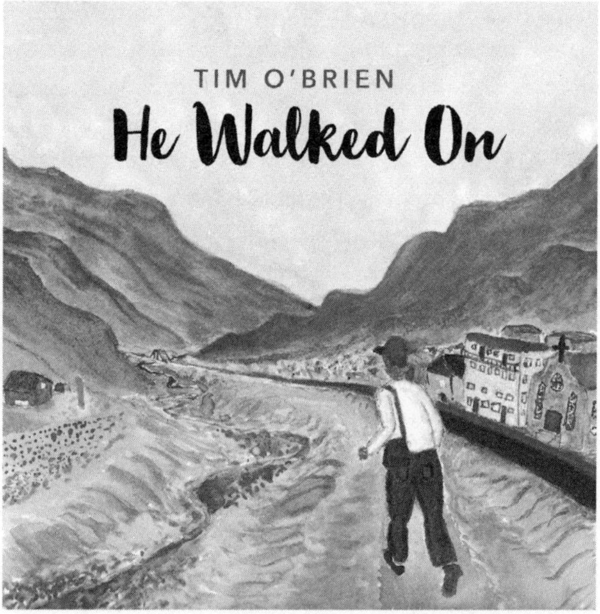

Album Cover Art, *He Walked On,* 2021. Courtesy Tim O'Brien.

Ultimately Kimbrough determined the online behavior crossed a line, and he uses the experience to highlight the value of moderation in political debate. "Politics ends up making laws. It's difficult work, and it's for people who are strong enough to know that if they didn't get their way 100 percent that they don't just storm out and leave. They have to sit there and try to make something work" (pers. interview, March 4, 2021).

Jesse Langlais points to a specific experience at a concert to illustrate welcoming divergent political beliefs in Town Mountain's audience. "I've seen it," Langlais says of a concert attendee who wore a "Make America Great Again" hat in support of Donald Trump while enjoying the music "standing next to somebody smoking weed" (pers. interview, August 20, 2021). Langlais doesn't see Town Mountain as a political band, but he sees this inclusivity as beautiful and notes the band welcomes it.

Rod Picott, alternatively, provides an illustration of subtlety rather than moderation or political even-handedness. He notes, "My own personal politics are in the stories, but I don't write political songs" (pers. interview, April 12, 2021). He similarly doesn't feel that his audience would characterize him as a political performer. Inspired by records such as Springsteen's *Nebraska,* which Picott says is "jam-packed with politics, but there's no politics. It's a story that tells you where he's coming from without telling you what to think. It's such a beautiful record in that way." Picott admits, "I'm basically a big lefty," but one has to really pay attention to his music and process the lyrics to see that. Indeed, blue-collar work-related themes characterize much of the music he writes, and Picott says that casual rather than contemplative listeners occasionally misattribute conservative political sentiment to him and his art.

Embracing the Political and Tackling Stereotypes

Embracing the political does not necessarily equate to embracing a partisan political stance, nor does it imply that artists push any given viewpoint. Embracing the political may mean these things, but it may also mean a willingness to address a singular issue, embrace ambiguity, and in many cases to actively challenge a variety of existing stereotypes.

Darrell Scott, who, as illustrated above, does not consider himself nor his music overtly political, provides a unique example of embracing an issue without broadly embracing partisan politics: he willingly takes on the coal industry in Appalachia in his music. This is very evident in "You'll Never Leave Harlan Alive" (1997) and his 2013 collaboration with Tim O'Brien, "Keep Your Dirty Lights On." The duo sings, "Every time they have elections, they talk how coal is clean. Well coal is cheap, but coal's still black and ain't never turning green," in the latter, Grammy-nominated song. Of his audience's relationship to the subject and their interpretation of him, Scott says that, while his audience likely does not fancy him a political performer, "They sure like my songs about coal" (pers. interview, April 21, 2021).

Reggie Harris's Underground Railroad program brings stories of slavery to children and youth from the sixth grade to college. The program seeks to provide a historical foundation and inspire inclusivity through song.[15] Harris recalls a mid-1990s Underground Railroad performance in Greenwich, Connecticut, where a lone Black woman was in attendance (pers. interview, August 24, 2021). The woman approached Harris after the program and said of his method of informing the predominately white and overwhelmingly affluent audience, "You went easy on them." Harris reports suggesting to the woman that there are multiple ways to deliver a point, and that a resonating argument doesn't always require a "sledgehammer." The idea is "to get access to make the points we need to make. . . . There are a lot of ways to make a point," Harris reasons.

Nevertheless, Harris notes that "white privilege makes [you] unprepared . . . to deal with what really happened" (pers. interview, August 24, 2021). Boatright-Horowitz, Marraccini, and Harps-Logan (2012) describe white privilege as the ability of whites to live free from structural obstacles related to skin color that prevent the same opportunities from reaching the Black community. Further, their research suggests that while some whites may be severely disadvantaged in life, those struggles do not leave them more capable of understanding racism: "To put it quite simply, no matter how difficult and seemingly underprivileged a white individual's life may seem to be, this individual is typically not required to deal with the daily effects of racism" (Boatright-Horowitz et al. 2012, 895). In turn, Harris feels that when African American artists such as himself perform for predominately white audiences, they must focus on learning and how to "lower the boom" of historical and on-going atrocities.

Harris also reports some pushback from the Black community. Regarding being characterized as "not Black enough," he says, "I would say I generally don't get a lot of inquiries by Black organizations [regarding performances]. . . . On some level they would say they understand that the programs I do are geared for informing white people" (pers. interview, August 24, 2021). Harris admits that when his audiences feature a relatively even racial mix or are predominately Black, while he still educates through song and story, there is a difference in the language used.

Slaid Cleaves, alternatively, reports that he perceives his audience to be coming from a similar perspective as him and, in turn, feels comfortable touching on politically laced issues. Cleaves first touched on the political in the 1980s with a song titled "Executive" while in a new wave band comprised of friends from southern Maine known as Still Missing. Cleaves describes the song as "a bitter screed against the executives who didn't think their shit stank. . . . It was that kind of punky attitude stuff" (pers. interview, February 24, 2021). Cleaves explains that, as his career evolved and he landed on the "folkie side of Americana," he began writing the "occasional workplace disaster song, the slightly political song, and the protest song." He is clear that he doesn't "take sides" or advocate partisan politics, but he often sings about the "little guy that takes down the big men" (pers. interview, September 9, 2021).

Rodney Crowell provides somewhat of a contrast to Cleaves, in that, rather than shifting from new age/punk bands, Crowell realized monumental success in contemporary country music as a solo artist and writing for others before settling in Americana. Indeed, several artists achieving varying levels of prominence in contemporary country have recorded songs written by Crowell. These artists include Gary Stewart, Lee Ann Womack, Wynonna Judd, Patty Loveless, and Emmylou Harris, who is also seen as a pioneer in Americana music.[16] Further illustrating Crowell's prolific songwriting status in more widely recognized genres, Rod Picott reminds, "Rodney wrote 'Shame on the Moon'" (pers. interview, April 12, 2021). Indeed, Bob Seger and the Silver Bullet Band's version of this song debuted at no. 40 on the Billboard Hot 100 chart and eventually ascended to no. 2.[17]

Despite this success, Crowell views Americana as a "more poetic offshoot of mainstream country" that permits room to grow thoughtfully. When asked if he sees Americana music as generally having a political message, Crowell says, "there is very little room in the mindset of contemporary country music for that kind of message, but there's tons in hip-hop and Americana" (pers. interview, March 3, 2021).

Crowell regularly underscores his appreciation for musical genres with African American roots. He educates when addressing the influence of jazz and blues. His appreciation for various musical styles can also be seen in the artists he consumes. "I'm a fan of Kendrick Lamar in the same way as [I am to] Duke Ellington to John Prine to Johnny Cash to the Beatles and Bob Dylan." Crowell says these artists are presenting a "message to think about" rather than a "product to sell." Thoughtful messages are key for Crowell, who says, "Look, I've had fifteen number one songs, but my audience isn't necessarily wanting to hear those songs. They're interested in the conversation I'm having with them."

As noted in the previous chapter, Crowell often challenges religion, and he has specifically addressed the gay community lyrically. The latter is a source of pride for Crowell. "I've had gay men in the audience tell me what that song means to them. . . . I'm very proud of that," he says of "Wandering Boy" (pers. interview, March 3, 2021). He is also proud of having produced

Rodney Crowell, taken on February 9, 2020, in Cayamo, Gulf of Mexico, aboard the *Norwegian Pearl.* Courtesy Michelle Stancil.

Chely Wright's 2010 *Lifted Off the Ground* album, which coincided with her publicly coming out as lesbian. "I was very instrumental in her coming out. I was with her every step of the way."[18]

In terms of overtly partisan political stances in his music, however, Crowell prefers to steer clear. "I'm also a realist. . . . I'm about as left as you can get, but the left has a whole lot to learn about communication. The same about the far right. They're going to have to move to the center to learn about themselves. . . . My far left leanings aren't going to do me any good if I can't talk to the other side" (pers. interview, March 3, 2021).

Eliza Gilkyson rationalizes how to integrate her leftist impulses in an extremely partisan and divided culture, much like Crowell. "I'm a political writer. . . . Well, I used to be a radical leftist, but I'm becoming a little bit more centrist because I think the left is starting to not be effective. . . . It's something that has impacted me a lot as a political writer. . . . There are easy issues you can talk about. . . . They're [not] about Empire or bringing soldiers in to buy into the American dream myth. . . . Honestly, there are easy ways to talk about political issues, but very few people are talking about patriarchal systems" (pers. interview, April 8, 2021).

For Gilkyson, patriarchy, misogyny, and racism are not being adequately addressed across musical spaces, but she recognizes the difficulty in doing so effectively. She sees Americana as successfully touching on key contemporary and historical material, but not diving deeply into structural and societal issues. She makes a distinction, however, for artists such as Patterson Hood and the Drive-By Truckers. "Their production is so fucking country-rockin' that a guy that's had a couple of beers" is going to be exposed to the message (pers. interview, April 8, 2021). She had a similar experience with her own "Highway 9" (2004), a track addressing US soldiers killing innocent civilians at a checkpoint in Iraq during the Bush administration. "Highway 9" begins, "Well the white god said to the little man we're gonna fulfill the scripture in the Holy Land. Between the Tigris and Euphrates it's a lot like hell. Go on and liberate my people and their O-I-L." The production of the song and the choral arrangement resulted in the track being played on trucker radio stations, according to Gilkyson. "That's one of the ways . . . through production that you can get [a political message] across with a really good chorus and hook line." She's careful to underscore, however, that people don't always "get it."

Gilkyson further cautions that while production might allow Americana artists to tread into controversial waters, barriers exist. "For folk singers like me [with overtly political lyrics], I can't get booked at an Americana festival. I'm way too far to the left" (pers. interview, April 8, 2021). Further, while she embraces leftist politics, her position on addressing contemporary politics is reminiscent of Tim O'Brien. "Now isn't the time to get message-y. It's a time to hold the line," she says in reference to music's place in Get Out the Vote efforts following Donald Trump's ousting in the 2020 presidential election.

Gilkyson, Patterson Hood, and Jamie Anderson are the most overtly political performers interviewed for this research. Hood repeatedly underscores the Drive-By Truckers' (DBT) desire to make political points and address social awareness. He looks outside Americana to hip-hop to make this point. "You know, it may not seem like it because none of us rap, but we've always been big fans. The hip-hop artists' approach to subject matter and how they approach particularly the political and social aspects of what they do has always been an influence on how we approach songwriting. . . . Our first album was called Gangstabilly for a reason" (pers. interview, February 19, 2021). Hood consistently refers to Outkast, rhythm and blues, and older country from the 1950s to the early 1970s as influences that not only impact DBT's musical style, but also content. "I thought if I can approach the kind of music influenced by the country stuff we've been listening to with the high-impact way of lyric-writing that the hip-hop artists of that era were doing, I thought it would be something interesting."

Hood addresses the content of DBT's *Dirty South* album as something of an illustration of how country artists can tackle darker lyrics without the same public pushback that hip-hop artists receive. "Country music is full of all these things (e.g., murder) that the hip-hop artists are rapping about. . . . It's been in country songs forever, but all of a sudden it's a big deal because this 'scary Black person' is doing it" (pers. interview, February 19, 2021). Certainly Hood's characterization illustrates the theory behind this research—music is often associated with racial stereotypes. His consideration of the duality of southern-ness touches also on this reality: "You can have both. You can have the same region that gave the world Otis Redding and Aretha Franklin and Booker T. and the M.G.'s and Faulkner and *To Kill a Mockingbird* and all these wonderful things also be a place that was really oppressive and has done some really terrible things to minorities as well as sometimes to ourselves. . . . Because we've also hurt ourselves with all of this hate and bullshit too."

Hood, like John Paul White, references his children when talking about DBT's trajectory and their willingness to hit contemporary politics head-on: "My kids know that during this time their dad stood for something, and it's something they agree with. . . . Everyone in our band, we all have kids and we're very concerned about what we're leaving to them" (pers. interview, February 19, 2021). Agreeing with a message is secondary for Hood, who sees the value in music expressing different viewpoints. "I didn't know what a Sandinista was until I heard the Clash. . . . [I was listening to] songs that were intellectually and politically way over my little redneck head, but I was always curious, so I wanted to see what was inspiring this great art." Hood

Patterson Hood at the Set Theatre in Kilkenny, Ireland, on May 2, 2011. Courtesy Nick Barber.

says music pushed him to learn and research a variety of viewpoints and see the value of ambiguity. He reports that he didn't always agree, but the import is in the learning. He brings this way of thinking into his own performances: "If you can make a handful of people each time out at least think about things on a little different slant, that's major. That's huge."

Jamie Anderson, who emphasizes that she came up through the women's music movement, also addresses social awareness in her music. Much of this emphasis is related to gender and sexual orientation. For instance, the first verse of Anderson's "I Wanna Be a Straight Guy" (1999) begins, "I wanna legally marry, I wanna make more money. I wanna feel safe wherever

I go, make a big noise when I blow my nose. I wanna wear an ugly tie, I wanna be a straight guy."

Beyond on-stage performances, Anderson is a scholar of women's music, having penned *An Army of Lovers: Women's Music of the Seventies and Eighties* (2019). This investigation of women's music doesn't portend to imply a specific genre or musical style. Rather, she looks to the evolution of this music that conveys the sentiments of the audience, which tend to be rooted in feminism and/or lesbianism.

"I'm an out lesbian and I'm sure they thought they'd pack the place with motorcycle dykes. They still buy drinks so I don't know why that would be a problem. It never happened, [but they were still concerned]," Anderson says of some venue owners when she was touring full time in the 1990s and 2000s (pers. interview, June 7, 2021). She says that the Americana medium always seemed to impart a message of diversity and inclusivity, but the artists have always been predominately heterosexual white men. Further, she says that she has "straight, middle-aged, white male performers" that are friends and are "big mouths" pushing venue owners to consider booking more female artists and artists of color, but she perceives them as a minority.

Anderson's characterization of the preponderance of diversity in messaging while Americana is generally dominated by straight white men is illustrative of Aengus Finnan's contention that the artists themselves can only do so much (pers. interview, May 18, 2021). Both artists see the onus on performers to solely account for diversity as somewhat misplaced, as folk and Americana artists tend to embrace diversity, but they are working within a culture that may be reticent to push political viewpoints and/or messages seen as extremely socially aware. Anderson reports that she typically played in venues that could be characterized as "straight" and she often found that there were enough "lefties" and gay people in the audience to make her comfortable; however, she has experienced several instances—including at the famous Bluebird Café in Nashville—where she did not feel welcome. "I've played venues where there were bomb threats," she reveals before noting that she has found audiences to be increasingly accepting (pers. interview, June 7, 2021).

Anderson also understandably notes that one can't expect straight white male artists to turn down gigs in the attempt to further push diversity. "You don't get anywhere if you don't wag your own tail in this business" (pers. interview, May 18, 2021). Thus, heterosexual white male artists are often in the position of endorsing and singing about diversity, but they aren't often in the position of creating diversity. John Paul White touched on this reality when referencing a neophyte performer being characterized as "another white guy." White says he understands, but he was also thinking, "Hey, that's me" (pers. interview, May 10, 2021).

Perhaps Cody Canada's discussion of his extreme ambivalence relating to his scheduled performance at a presidential inaugural event in 2016 is the most appropriate place to conclude a discussion of music and politics. "I was signed up to play Black Tie and Boots, and when Trump won I backed out. I said no. I'm not doing this . . . I don't care who's there. I can't stand behind this person. It was not me going out of my way to be political. . . . It doesn't come down to being Democratic or Republican or liberal or wherever you're at. It comes down to being a good human being. I felt like Obama was a great human being and we needed somebody else like that and we got the opposite" (pers. interview, March 29, 2021). While Canada's reasoning was clear, he notes that his "band and crew were already through TSA at the airport and [I'm] on my front porch pacing and smoking," struggling with the decision because he had originally agreed to perform.

Canada wrote "Sam Hain" (2018) as a result of the experience. The chorus states, "Well they're boarding up the windows, locking all the doors, wiping all the shelves of the grocery stores. Banging on your drum as you're marching us to war." "Look where we were a couple years later," Canada says of Trump's response to the COVID-19 pandemic (pers. interview, March 29, 2021).

Canada and his wife, Shannon, operate a School of Rock franchise, and he reports that two of their instructors were threatened online following Trump parades in New Braunfels, Texas, simply because they were African American. This was particularly bothersome to Canada, who has endeavored to cultivate a diverse audience from his time with Cross Canadian Ragweed to the present by choosing songs with inclusive lyrics (e.g., covering Will Kimbrough's "Betty Was Black [and Willie Was White]") and featuring people of color as supporting musicians.

Gender/Racial Differences

When considering a comprehensive list of artists interviewed for this research, John Paul White, Aengus Finnan, and Bernice Lewis commented that the sample was male-heavy and generally lacking in artists of color. These observations are accurate. As previously reported, the response rate among women performers was lower than that of their male counterparts. In turn, only six women participated in this research. Likewise, there are only two participating artists of color (one male and one female) and only one artist, a woman, identifying as nonheterosexual. The result is seven participants who are not heterosexual white male artists. This general lack of diversity leads to two questions. First, why were female artists and artists of color less likely to respond to requests to participate in this research? Second, do women and minorities in this musical space discuss diversity in a manner different from white men?

The first question is essentially unanswerable. Artists do not generally share personal contact information publicly. To that end, initial communication was typically made by email to managers, agents, and publicists.[19] Unknown senders' messages are often filtered into junk mail (spam, trash, etc.), lessening the likelihood that the initial email or second attempts to contact were seen. Additionally, as managers, agents, and publicists act as clearinghouses for artists, the possibility that multiple requests for participation failed to reach the intended artist(s) exists. Third, initial communication was made during the worldwide COVID-19 pandemic, when artists were not touring and, in turn, may not have actively been responding to press requests unless new albums were scheduled for release. Similarly, childcare of school-age children during the pandemic could have disproportionately affected female artists. All of these explanations could also apply to white male artists, however.

To the second question posed above, slight differences can be seen between the female artists and artists of color and the participating white men. The interviewed artists, including the white men, overwhelmingly see the need for greater diversity within American roots music and are emphatic about their desire to grow diversity in their own audiences.[20] The distinction between the women and minorities interviewed can be seen in the manner of addressing what they perceive as lack of diversity in this musical space, however.

Jamie Anderson, Eliza Gilkyson, and Bernice Lewis all point to the difficulty female artists face in securing gigs. Anderson says, "I've been told by venue owners, 'We booked a woman last week'" (pers. interview, June 7,

2021). Reggie Harris reports a similar experience with artists of color. While he is sought after for educational programming, he sees festival organizers as essentially looking to fill racial and gender quotas with performers (pers. interview, August 24, 2021). When a minimal level of gender and racial diversity is achieved through booking, organizers and venue owners return to the white male artists they are confident their audiences expect.

"We don't get as many gigs as [some of the men you've interviewed]. . . . You get good by doing, and we don't do it as much. . . . In terms of honing our craft or becoming a proficient accompanist, we have had limited opportunities. There's absolutely no substitute for stage time," Bernice Lewis contends (pers. interview, May 25, 2021). She speculates that the difficulty for women to find and maintain an audience may be exacerbated by several factors, including spousal and/or child-rearing responsibilities, and points to having been characterized as different. "What's different is that I'm a woman," Lewis reasons.

BettySoo recognizes that she's different because of her gender and Korean heritage (pers. interview, September 21, 2021). She recognizes that being an Asian American sets her apart from other artists in this space and often leaves audiences and journalists focusing on her race. Regarding her appreciation for country music, BettySoo notes that while she identifies as Asian American, she grew up listening to country music in "Spring, Texas, where Lyle Lovett was the hometown hero." To that end, she wasn't different than childhood contemporaries, but observers focus on demographic characteristics that signal difference rather that broad cultural influences that impact individuals across races/ethnicities.

Nevertheless, Kristen Englenz reports that she finds Americana to be a very inclusive space even if dominated by heterosexual white men (pers. interview, July 27, 2021). Englenz, who characterizes much of her music as rooted in the experience of young, independent women rather than being political, is also emphatic that Americana provides artists with opportunities to incorporate social awareness into music whether subtly or more overtly that popular music does not provide. Further, Eliza Gilkyson specifically points to female artists like Brandi Carlile "moving the ball down the court, and I'm kind of impressed" (pers. interview, April 8, 2021).

WDVX music director Nelson Gullett concurs with Englenz that Americana provides a venue in which artists can stretch more comfortably than

Eliza Gilkyson in Santa Fe, New Mexico, in 2011.
Courtesy Seth Roffman.

popular and/or more commercial musical spaces provide, given the often formulaic approach necessary to be commercially successful (pers. interview, September 16, 2021).[21] He speculates that, given the general historical prevalence of white men in Americana and the way in which certain white male audience members take to social media to criticize women and minorities, women may feel more guarded regarding providing their thoughts publicly outside of lyrics than established male artists may be. Gullett is quick to note, however, that male artists are generally very supportive of their female peers, and that female artists such as Margo Price and Emma Swift "can give as good as they get in most instances."

Summary

This chapter summarizes the thoughts of participating Americana artists. The sample is comprised of artists that identify with the Americana label primarily as well as those that first identify with constituent genres, such as country, folk, or rock. The sample is similarly diverse in age and acclaim. Alternatively, white heterosexual men dominate the sample.

This group can be characterized as contemplative and moderate to liberal in their personal political philosophies. The artists that addressed political activism can also be said to collectively support Get Out the Vote efforts regardless of partisanship and ideology, and even those with strong political opinions see the value in moderation and tolerance of alternate opinions. Their approaches to addressing politics and/or social awareness in their lyrics and/or performances are varied, however. Contributing artists, such as Colin Gilmore and Jesse Langlais, prefer to avoid overtly political messaging, while others prefer to tackle it directly.

The collective group can also be said to be both aware of and concerned about the status of women and minorities in Americana. All wish to see greater diversity, but the women and minority artists participating in this research were generally more willing to explain and speculate about why the diversity gap exists in a medium that promotes messages of inclusivity.

›››››› 4 ‹‹‹‹‹‹

THE COMMUNITY

Robbie Fulks describes "That's Where I'm From" (2013) as being about a man, not himself, living in a quiet suburb reflecting on his roots.[1] "A man climbs as high as he can, but his heart belongs where it began. I can see in my mind's eye, a shack on a hillside, and a mean billy goat on a chain. And Dad doin' battle with dirt hard as gravel. And summers the crops never came." While the constituent genres of Americana music have varied roots, such as the rurality expressed in the Fulks song, one could argue that Americana has evolved from the radio format pioneered by *Honky Tonk Amnesia* and the Americana charts to a unique culture that extends beyond the artists and lyrics and into the behaviors and attitudes of audiences. In fact, what could collectively be considered humble origins may have evolved into a community that doesn't consistently reflect the characters that historically occupy prominence in the music—at least not in terms of socioeconomic demographics.

I recounted to BettySoo an experience in a Jacksonville, Florida, supermarket parking lot in which I saw a bumper sticker that read, "Remember in November, Donald Trump killed John Prine." When I struck up a conversation with the owners of the vehicle, I found that they, too, were disappointed with the relative lack of roots music in northeastern Florida. BettySoo saw the experience as an illustration of the broader Americana culture "getting it" (pers. interview, September 21, 2021). "It's just perfect because that's something he would have said," she says of Prine. BettySoo further wonders if the audience, which she characterizes as, for the most part, similar to the artists in political leanings and demography, enjoys being somewhat outside of the mainstream, and potentially considers themselves more socially

Robbie Fulks at McGonigel's Mucky Duck in Houston, Texas, on August 14, 2015. Courtesy Nick Barber.

aware than fans of more popular music. Robbie Fulks similarly sees parallels between artists and audience: "You look at the fans and you think they're like me, for better or for worse" (pers. interview, April 19, 2021).

This chapter draws from artist interviews as well as interviews with music journalists/personalities and festival organizers/nonprofit executive directors that work across constituent genres of the Americana format or within a single genre to provide a view of the Americana community. To that end, a consideration of culture is offered before presenting a demographic assessment of the audience and a consideration of the content of audience beliefs/attitudes relating to government, politics, and social awareness. A return to the broader implications of the Americana culture concludes the chapter.

While the analysis of the audience is based on secondary data collection, it nevertheless points to the similarities between artist and audience expressed by BettySoo and Robbie Fulks while also underscoring the element of elitism noted in previous chapters. It is imperative, however, prior to unfolding the discussion of community, to underscore that elitism and/or social awareness are not synonymous with formal education. While artists often conceive of their fans as well-educated, they are also careful to note that many fans may not be college educated. This fan base, regardless of level of formal education, has a firm grasp of social and political events and outcomes that is not characteristic of Americans more generally. Artists, journalists, and others interviewed for this research likewise see the audience as overwhelmingly socially conscious.

Ultimately this chapter points to the need to consider Americana as more than a radio format or even a musical genre. Rather, Americana is a culture characterized by the music. The music, in turn, signals association with the culture to those knowledgeable. Colin Gilmore summarizes this well by stating, "I do believe that music is a healing force, and it creates community" (pers. interview, December 21, 2021). Therefore, an underlying question grows more prominent as this chapter unfolds: Those within the culture "get it," but do those outside the culture fall back on existing stereotypes (i.e., hippies and cowboys) when they do not?

The Roots Music Culture

Much of the discussions of roots music generally and Americana specifically addressed herein presume the reader has a foundational knowledge of what culture is. Perhaps a broad discussion of culture is necessary to advance this narrative, however. Kluckhohn's (1951, 86) seminal definition posits, "Culture consists in patterned ways of thinking, feeling and reacting, acquired and transmitted mainly by symbols, constituting the distinctive achievements of human groups, including their embodiments in artifacts; the essential core of culture consists of traditional (i.e., historically derived and selected) ideas and especially their attached values." This particularly verbose approach to defining culture may be historically important and apt, but it lacks the concision necessary for understanding the Americana culture. Hofstede's (2001, 5) more contemporary contention that culture is "the collective programming of the mind that distinguishes the members of one group or category of people from another" provides that concision. Importantly, Hofstede's approach considers groups as varied as those based in region and ethnicity to those based in age. Similarly, Inglehart (1997, 15) succinctly explains that culture is "a system of attitudes, values, and knowledge that is widely shared within a society."

Whether one prefers the Kluckhohn (1951), Hofstede (2001), or Inglehart (1997) definition, the key to moving forward in understanding the Americana culture is not to deconstruct these characterizations and dispute the minutia that contrasts them, but rather to focus on the similarities that allow us to understand precisely what culture is. In other words, what is the widely shared mental programming that constitutes the "essential core" of the Americana audience?

Aengus Finnan underscores the desire for personal narrative through songwriting and storytelling as well as the simple nature of "the music of the people" in addressing the cultural ethos surrounding roots music. "Harry Belafonte, Pete Seeger, or any of the folk legends and Americana troubadours, you don't have to be literally sitting in the city, the town, or the state... that you're writing about. The craft of an artist is to be able to observe and listen and pick-up.... Gordon Lightfoot wasn't on the *Edmund Fitzgerald*. He read about it in the paper and he felt the story, but he wrote that song. He wasn't in the riots in Detroit, but he wrote 'Black Day in July,' which was banned on most of the radio [stations] in the US.... Part of the work of an artist, whether they call themselves a folk singer, or a singer-songwriter, or an Americana artist, is to observe and reflect and to share" (pers. interview, May 18, 2021). Finnan further speaks to the value of the honesty in this art by activating a broader cultural sentiment: "The heartstrings of regional-based songs resonate at a national level."

Joel Rafael explains his role in relaying this heartful societal impression of roots music: "What I do personally... is just to continue to wage the struggles that will always be waged for humanity because every government, every form of government... have all violated the basic human rights that people are born with... the basic freedoms that we should have as children of the earth" (pers. interview, April 26, 2021). Rafael further addresses the connection between this intrinsic freedom-based view of the music and the roots music audience: "We don't expect our audience to be big. It's never been big. People that do what we do have never had large audiences, but the fight goes on . . . because there's always those forces of oppression."

The broader roots music/Americana community that seeks out this reflective music that conveys struggle and the "common man's" experience also seeks out the welcoming environments that provide it. They share an appreciation for the varied "common men," an honest (even if not personal) account of related experiences, and a welcoming environment with like-minded contemporaries.

Like-minded contemporaries are best considered through BettySoo's "people who get it" lens. The artists and audiences in American roots music seek genuine stories and emotion, but that doesn't require personal experience with content. For example, when Tim O'Brien sings "He Walked On," the knowledgeable roots music consumer would likely realize that O'Brien is far too young to have joined John Lewis on Bloody Sunday in Selma, Alabama, while also understanding both Lewis's role in the civil rights movement and O'Brien's appreciation for Lewis.[2] Likewise, the audience need not identify as southern and/or African American to appreciate the messaging.

The Lewis-O'Brien example is characteristic of the Americana community's high level of historical/political sophistication and shared political tolerance. These shared traits are addressed at length below, following a consideration of observable demographic trends across the Americana audience. Importantly, these demographic identifiers both promote messages of inclusivity and contribute to the stereotype that prevents wider circulation of those messages.

Observing the Roots Music Audience

Locating a point of origin to address the Americana audience is nearly as difficult as broadly identifying the origins of the various constituent genres of roots music. Fortunately, the purpose of this research is less concerned with chronicling the growth of the Americana audience and centers on the contemporary roots music audience. Slaid Cleaves characterizes fans of both this music broadly and his music specifically as "folks that don't recognize themselves in the broader popular culture. . . . People on the edges of culture" (pers. interview, February 24, 2021). Understanding these individuals requires a consideration of who they are demographically as well as their expectations of this musical space.

Aengus Finnan discusses the onset of his tenure at Folk Alliance International as executive director as "a time when the board really wanted to get past [a point where] Folk Alliance was stuck in this place where it was washed out with white guys with guitars as the only definition of folk music. . . . And, I was one of them . . . but what it didn't represent was folk music as music of the people" (pers. interview, May 18, 2021). This is illustrative of the conundrum artists and other professionals in roots music face. Specifically, while they may endeavor to be inclusive, impediments such as stereotypes and institutionalized roadblocks in the forms of location and delivery of music are difficult to navigate. Finnan points to various roots musics as the "music of the people"—people who are culturally diverse and who have gotten lost in broader conceptualizations of North American musical culture, which has been dominated by white, male singer-songwriters.

Rodney Crowell points to these types of institutional roadblocks impacting the composition of his audience by considering his successful early career. "I'm a white guy that came up through the country ranks. [I was] Culturally not on the radar [outside of contemporary country]" (pers. interview, March 3, 2021). Crowell discusses a moment at a show in Houston while singing "Don't Get Me Started," which addresses issues relating to American culture, the Middle East, and corporate greed, when he saw an evident change in his audience. "Some were bright-eyed and smiling and some were startled. I want to be careful and not contribute to the divide, but at the same time [I don't want to] betray my message or sensibilities." While Crowell's transition to Americana facilitated inclusive lyrics and led to a new, more contemplative segment of his audience, he hasn't seen a similar shift in the racial or generational composition, which he characterizes as predominately white men and women in their early forties to late sixties, with a smattering of younger attendees.

Like Crowell, Eliza Gilkyson characterizes her fan base as primarily forty-five and above, and the forty-plus age range is echoed by many of the artists interviewed for this volume (pers. interview, April 8, 2021). Rod Picott, who was fifty-six when interviewed for this research, says his audience "tends to be even older than I am" (pers. interview, April 12, 2021). Will Kimbrough jokes of his audience's age, "forty to eighty, if they're still around" (pers. interview, March 4, 2021). Kimbrough clarifies that the age range of his audience may be explained by audiences looking for something that "looks like them" (pers. interview, March 4, 2021). Colin Gilmore also gauges his audience as mid-forties or older, which he sees as making sense given the roots music audience and his being influenced by such artists as Buddy Holly, The Clash, Townes Van Zandt, and his father Jimmie Dale Gilmore/The Flatlanders, who preceded him by decades (pers. interview, December 21, 2021). Nevertheless, even younger artists, such as Kristen Englenz and Anana Kaye, report a preponderance of older fans at their performances. Notably, Englenz reports that she thinks her "at home" audience may be older than those attending live performances (pers. interview, July 27, 2021).

Likewise music director and host Nelson Gullett informs me that a common characterization of the Americana audience is "fifty to death" (pers. interview, September 16, 2021). Jon Bernstein of *Rolling Stone* reports that the aging crowd may be something Americana has to contend with in the future to sustain viable audiences (pers. interview, March 17, 2021). Nevertheless, several of the artists interviewed (i.e., Cody Canada, Slaid Cleaves, Jesse Langlais, RB Morris, Tim O'Brien, and Darrell Scott) report families attending their respective live performances, and Mary Muse, executive director of the Kerrville Folk Festival, says families with young children are in regular attendance at the festival (pers. interview, March 23, 2021). "I've seen some of them since they were in diapers."

Each artist interviewed, including the two participating non-white artists, echoed the primarily white audience. When asked whether her Korean heritage translates into greater Asian American attendance at her performances, BettySoo explains that her Asian American fans understandably likely do not want to attend only to be asked if they're drawn to her because of her background. "If anything, they might want to stay home [to avoid it]," she laughs (pers. interview, September 21, 2021).

Darrell Scott summarizes the general sentiment of most artists interviewed for this research regarding race and the Americana audience: they're "largely white, but I don't know how to fix that" (pers. interview, April 21, 2021). Likewise, Slaid Cleaves says, "They're not diverse. It's a very white audience, which is weird to me because I tend to think my songs could relate to anyone, but I guess that's short-sighted of me" (pers. interview, February 24, 2021).

The reflectiveness of Scott and Cleaves is characteristic of most artists, the festival organizers, and the journalists contributing to this research. The

Bernice Lewis at the Kerrville Folk Festival in Kerrville, Texas, on May 27, 2018. Courtesy Neale Eckstein.

desire to reach a diverse and inclusive audience is ever-present in this space. Artists generally feel it is incumbent on them to diversify their audiences, but the journalists and one of the festival organizers/nonprofit executive directors specifically looked to the broader roots music culture as responsible for representing homes for all versions of the "common man." Aengus Finnan explains that even if radio stations and local music venues are featuring the best of folk music or the best of Americana music, the art tends to unfold in a white-dominated space. Moreover, he explains that indigenous artists and artists with racial/ethnic minority backgrounds may be expected to play to group-based stereotypes (pers. interview, May 18, 2021). In turn, thrusting the onus of growing diversity purely on artists is short-sighted.

Reggie Harris's characterization of his audience likely identifies them as the most racially diverse of interviewed artist fan bases. Nevertheless, while he reports that he occasionally performs for racially diverse and/or majority Black audiences, whites are the dominant racial group regularly in attendance at his performances (pers. interview, August 24, 2021). The characterization of Harris's fan base as majority white is particularly noteworthy given that much of his music, and indeed his career, has emphasized the role of diverse racial/ethnic/religious groups in achieving measures of

Robert Greer (guitar) and Jesse Langlais (banjo) of Town Mountain at Zanzabar in Louisville, Kentucky, on March 4, 2022. Courtesy Jay Strausser.

equality in the United States. "It's never been by one group," Harris says of American struggles for civil rights (pers. interview, August 24, 2021).

Jesse Langlais of Town Mountain, Cody Canada, and John Paul White also point to diversity in their respective audiences, but Langlais qualifies that his characterization of Town Mountain's audience is relative to other forms of roots music. "I look out at a Town Mountain audience and see demographs from all walks of life. I see a little bit of everybody out there. Not all bands have that. . . . When it falls into the parameters of roots music it slims up a bit" (pers. interview, August 20, 2021). White further describes his fan base as quite diverse in terms of regional dispersion, education, age, and race (pers. interview, May 10, 2021). Nevertheless, he states that the perception is overwhelmingly white (as discussed in the previous chapter).

Colin Gilmore further sees venue as important in establishing community, and specifically addresses age with regard to house concerts (pers. interview, December 21, 2021). He says he performs better when playing in locations where the expectation is "We're going to go listen to some music together." He specifically points to venues such as the Mucky Duck in Houston and The Ark in Ann Arbor before turning to the virtue of house concerts.[3]

"It takes a community to get a bunch of people to all gather in one place. Usually the host of a well-done house concert has a community that really trusts their taste and trusts that at least they're going to come and have a good time. [The hosts] foster this [community], they take donations . . . and they give it all to the artist[s]." Gilmore says these hosts are often people who are approximately his age (forty-six at the time of the interview) or older who want to consume the music in a comfortable environment without the "smoky bar" atmosphere, "A lot of them have kids. A lot of them are done with driving to a downtown location and trying to find parking. . . . It tends to be really great for the artist and the crowd, and the hosts are generally doing a great service. You know, making a sacrifice they don't get monetary reward for. They get the pleasure of hearing the music and putting the crowd together. Other than that, they work hard just to make this thing happen."

Jon Bernstein's discussion of City Winery in New York City illustrates how race may overlap with age and venue in Americana.[4] "That model has really fascinated me. . . . For someone like a Rodney Crowell, City Winery is where you'd usually go to see him in New York. [It's where] a lot of these singer-songwriters—sort of ritzy, Americana, southern—singer-songwriters are playing especially if they're over the age of thirty/forty. It's very clear who that space is for. . . . The shows aren't inordinately expensive, actually. You can see Rodney Crowell there for $35, but you know you're encouraged to sit down and order a $15 glass of wine and the $25 pizza" (pers. interview, March 17, 2021). Bernstein further describes City Winery as "A very white space . . . and, it's a very cosmopolitan space." He perceives this type of experience as "emblematic of the way roots music has presented itself" and the audience it attracts. "Probably the cheapest shorthand is like the NPR audience, right?" (pers. interview, March 17, 2021).

Political Ideology and Political Tolerance

The "NPR crowd" and "country music for Democrats" descriptions of the audience and music respectively are important to an accurate understanding of the Americana culture. While the artists, organizers, and journalists participating in this research recognize that the applicability of those descriptors is imperfect, they nevertheless understand the culture as empathetic toward the "common man," broadly socially aware, and possessing a minimal awareness of a degree of validity in a liberal political ideology if not the full-blown embracing of progressive political ideology. In summarizing the Americana community, Tim O'Brien is clear that while there are varying political attitudes among artists and fans, the "Country music for Democrats" characterization is apt. "That's what it is," O'Brien laughs (pers. interview, February 24, 2021).

Patterson Hood provides an illustration of an overwhelmingly liberal preference in his audience. He sees this as a shift from the onset of DBT and has embraced the ideology he sees the band as sharing with most of the current audience. "I always loved the idea of a Willie Nelson concert being so democratic. . . . I had it in my head that maybe that would be our future. I was really proud of how diverse our crowd was—at least diverse among white people. . . . But, after *American Band* (2016) we did run a lot of those people off, but we also had a lot of new people come on board and the basic mix of the crowd I like better. . . . To put it bluntly, there was a lot less assholery in the crowd" (pers. interview, February 19, 2021). Of the disruptive element that Hood saw as "ruining others' good times," starting fights, and playing contrarian to DBT's politically progressive messaging, "I don't want to play for a bunch of assholes. I don't want their money. If they feel that way, if they think what Trump was doing and things like what happened at the capital this year, if they think that's okay, I don't want them. . . . It's almost like taking blood money. I can donate it to a liberal cause, but I'd honestly just rather not see them, rather not have them there. If that makes me an asshole, I'm okay with it. . . . I'm more worried about what my kids think about me at the end of the day than what some guy who don't even know how to put on his hat in the correct direction [thinks of me]. . . . If his hat's looking back, he's probably more into looking backwards than forwards." Hood sees the contemporary Drive-By Truckers crowd as forward-looking.

Alternatively, Rod Picott, who identifies as liberal, speculates that some of his fan base perceives him to be more conservative and may likewise identify as conservative. Picott illustrated an experience with an attendee to his performance in a library series in Ringwood, New Jersey, in 2003 following the release of his first two albums. Picott describes the attendee as a young, somewhat feminine man that seemed to "fight retreating into himself" (pers. interview, April 12, 2021). Picott says the man admitted that he was unsure whether Picott and his audience would be welcoming to someone like him. Picott reports being saddened by the experience, but explains that he understood the young man's trepidation: "There is a profoundly masculine element to those first few albums, but it had not entered my consciousness that an audience feels a relationship to the performer via the work—I was a neophyte. It was a bit of a profound realization to understand a listener sometimes connects the singer directly to the material. That for the listener, there is often no distance between the person and the work" (pers. interview, November 11, 2021).

BettySoo similarly perceives elements of ideological inconsistency in Americana audiences. She specifically points to an evident conservative group of bluegrass listeners (pers. interview, November 27, 2021). "There's a big chunk of the traditional bluegrass audience I've observed that can hold views that would seem strange bedfellows." She specifically offers the pro-union anti-climate segment of that population before addressing specific artists' audiences. She notes that James McMurtry and Ray Wylie Hubbard have satirical lyrics in some songs that stand in stark contrast to how right-leaning audiences may perceive them. BettySoo states, "No matter how literary the writing, . . . when satire is taken literally, well, you know what happens."

She specifically refers to McMurtry's "Choctaw Bingo" (2002) and Ray Wylie Hubbard's "Up Against the Wall, Redneck Mother" (1973) as examples of satire that have been misinterpreted by right-leaning fans. Seely (2014) refers to the former as a "Midwestern meth head masterpiece."[5] Lyrics include, "And he stopped off in Tushka at the pop Knife and Gun place. Bought a SKS rifle and a couple full cases of that steel core ammo with the Berdan primers from some East bloc nation that no longer needs 'em. And a Desert Eagle, that's one great big ole pistol. I mean .50 caliber made by bass-ass Hebrews. And some surplus tracers for that old BAR of Slaton's."

Regarding "Up Against the Wall, Redneck Mother," Hubbard explained, "it was meant to be satire and irony, mocking rednecks at the time. . . . The thing is, not everybody gets it. Jerry Jeff recorded it and all of a sudden you had these rednecks in cowboy hats and 'America—Love it or Leave it' T-shirts singing along with it."[6] "Up Against the Wall, Redneck Mother" lyrics include, "Well, you know, he sure likes to drink that Lone Star beer. And he chases it down with Wild Turkey bourbon liquor. He's got a '57 GMC pick-up truck with a gun rack. And a 'I'd rather be a roper than a doper' bumper sticker."

Based on the Hood and Picott examples as well as BettySoo's insights, "leftist" and "liberal" may not consistently apply to the entire Americana audience and/or all artists. Certainly, artists interviewed in this volume have noted the presence of ideologically right-leaning and/or Republican fans even though those individuals do not constitute a majority (or even a sizeable minority). In turn, highly politically tolerant is a more accurate description.

Political tolerance is a difficult concept to define. Indeed, scholars tend to define political tolerance by inferring what it is not. Studies in political tolerance tend to focus on perception of intolerance (e.g., Stouffer's 1995 seminal piece) or measures, such as reactions to least-like groups (e.g., Gibson 1992; Sullivan, Piereson, and Marcus 1979; Sullivan, Piereson, and Marcus 1982), which similarly get at the antithesis of tolerance.[7] Specifically, Sullivan, Piereson, and Marcus (1982, 4) define political tolerance as "a willingness to 'put up with' things that one rejects." In turn, we can reasonably presume that tolerance is characterized by an absence or relative low degree of negative antipathy toward given groups and a willingness to entertain and/or see validity in viewpoints and people with whom you disagree. Each contributor to this research could be characterized as politically tolerant based on this conceptualization. Similarly, all would characterize the broader Americana culture in this regard.

Chart 4.1 is used to illustrate the relationship between the Americana audience/culture and political tolerance, where the x-axis represents level of political liberalism and the y-axis represents one's willingness to entertain viewpoints contrary to one's own predispositions (i.e., level of political tolerance). Based on the interviews collected in this research, the general Americana audience can be characterized as falling into the gray-shaded quadrants signifying Willing-Conservative, Willing-Liberal, and Unwilling-Liberal. Darker gray shading signifies dominance. Notably, contributors to this research suggest that some involved in this culture can be characterized as somewhat conservative; however, Americana fans are not likely to fall into the Unwilling-Conservative quadrant. In other words, Americana fans tend to be tolerant and/or liberal. They are less likely to be conservative and unlikely to be intolerant.

Will Kimbrough's "My Right Wing Friend" (2020) explicitly puts political tolerance to music with lyrics reflective of the Prine-related bumper sticker addressed at the onset of this chapter. "For a time we left off poli-

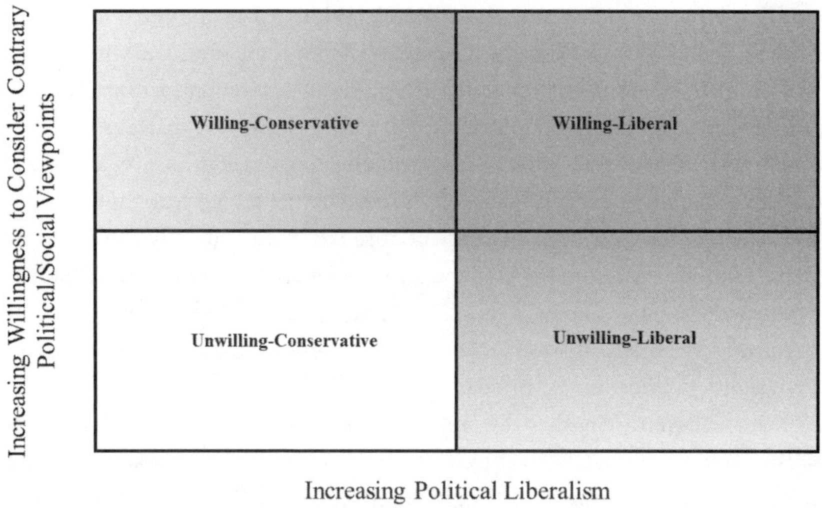

Chart 4.1. Tolerance-Ideology Typology

tics and we screwed down tight the lid. Took our families on vacation to the beautiful Blue Ridge. Laughing, drinking, hiking, nighttime, cold beers in the fridge. Happy memories of a way back when. My right wing friend. So here we are in 2020 social distancing. Trump is in the White House. Ain't life a funny thing. And when the virus took John Prine, we cried there goes my every everything. Now we are all Sam Stones—alone with our balloons. I guess I'll always love you. Though my views will always rub you."[8]

"My Right Wing Friend" also humanizes individuals and points to a potential extension of political tolerance—empathy/group empathy (e.g., Sullivan, Pierson, and Marcus 1982). Group empathy is particularly related to this research, as it is measured by capturing feelings of concern and perspective toward groups. For example, Sirin, Valentino, and Villalobos (2017) utilize respondents' level of identification with the statement "I often have tender, concerned feelings for people from another racial or ethnic group who are less fortunate than me" in their "Group Empathy Index" (GEI).[9] Sirin, Villalobos, and Valentino (2016, 2021) also illustrate that empathy toward outgroups (those with which one does not identify) can affect policy attitudes. In turn, empathy impacts attitudes toward minority groups (e.g., racial/ethnic minorities, the LGBTQ+ community) by those not identifying as members of those groups. If "My Right Wing Friend" illustrates tolerance and empathy, Lucinda Williams explicitly tackles a *lack* of empathy in "East Side of Town" (2014). "You got your ideas and your visions. And you say you sympathize. You look but you don't listen. There's no empathy in your eyes."

Artists and other contributors to this research did not speak as much to the degree of group empathy held by members of the community as whole, but several contributors addressed the concept in such a way that one can see inspiring empathy as a thematic undercurrent. Specifically, Aengus Finnan's desire to reorganize FAI to recognize all forms of folk music as "music of the people," Slaid Cleaves's and Rod Picott's writing from the perspective of the downtrodden and overlooked, and Joel Rafeal's decades-long focus on civil rights provide apt examples.

Tim O'Brien provides the most obvious example, however. I asked O'Brien about a partially obscured sign beneath a small American flag I saw in the background of a video performance of "Sod Buster" featuring Jan Fabricius.[10] He shared a photo of the sign. It remains in his home and ostensibly was created to resemble a campaign yard sign promoting candidate "Frank Empathy."[11] O'Brien explains that he saw the sign on a neighbor's yard and searched online for an explanation. Upon finding the related website (frankempathy.com) which states "The goal of this 'campaign' is simple: to prompt conversations and thoughts about empathy," O'Brien contacted the artists. "The sign was on our lawn much of last year," O'Brien adds (pers. interview, September 8, 2021).

Colin Gilmore characterized the greater Americana community as empathic, and states that he's hopeful he can contribute to that sense through his music. "Even though I don't think of my music as very direct in the way of social attitudes toward each other . . . I would like for my music to affect people in a way that they look at each other and go 'Okay, we both felt something from that. Maybe we need to look out for each other a bit'" (pers. interview, December 21, 2021). Gilmore says he's confident that he's oftentimes able to have this effect and takes particular pleasure in being approached by racially and ethnically diverse performance attendees who convey appreciation for the music and the overall sentiment: "If I feel like I've fostered a sense of community, then I feel like I've done the right thing."

Despite a community that can be characterized as high in political tolerance as well as high in empathy, contributors are aware that a visible minority of this fan base could be characterized as less supportive of women,

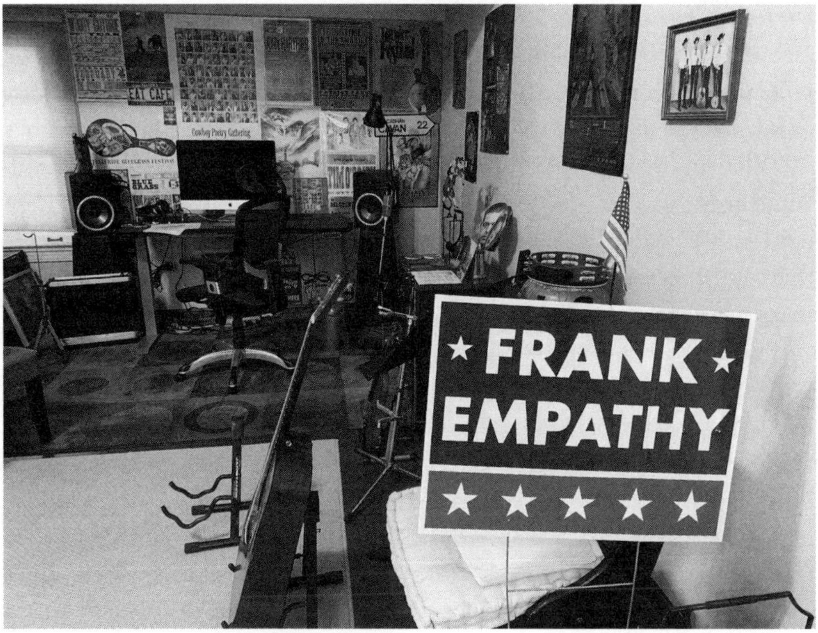

Frank Empathy artwork by Doug Brumley and Jason West. Photo taken by Tim O'Brien. Courtesy Doug Brumley, Jason West, and Tim O'Brien.

and that institutional impediments in the form of racial and anti-LGBTQ+ stereotypes persist. Therefore, empathy may at times be absent and political intolerance can infiltrate Americana culture despite artists' inclination to embrace diversity and inclusivity. Jamie Anderson's observation of LGBTQ+ comfort in Americana provides an apt illustration: "Even in Americana, it can take courage to come out" (pers. interview, September 28, 2021).

Authenticity

Both Eliza Gilkyson and Bernice Lewis poignantly illustrate that they have experienced difficulty finding and maintaining a fan base in the American south. Lewis is a mainstay at the Kerrville Folk Festival in Texas, but otherwise does not regularly tour the South. Likewise, Gilkyson, who is from California and identifies as urban, states of Americana in the South, "I think if I had authentic southern roots myself I'd fit into the club, but I just don't" (pers. interview, April 8, 2021). She further states of her decision to no longer tour in the southern United States, "I don't really want to change what I do. I'd rather push the things that are important to me because there are a lot of people doing a great job of this."[12] This consideration of authenticity to self and music can be seen across the artists interviewed in this volume.

Will Kimbrough describes the exchange between songwriter and audience through a lens of authenticity. He specifically points to the skill Rodney Crowell and Todd Snider have respectively in making this connection to their audiences. Kimbrough describes the audience as searching for something "authentic" and "real" (pers. interview, March 4, 2021).

On why authenticity seems to be so key in Americana, Rod Picott underscores that songwriters occupy center stage in this musical space. "There's a really easy answer for that. . . . The acts that are working in the Americana field are songwriters. They write their own material, so there's a really close connection to who they are on stage even though it might be a distilled [version of themselves]. It's a distillation, but it's still you. . . . In other genres of music, that doesn't even come into the question" (pers. interview, April 12, 2021).

Aengus Finnan also emphasizes the ability of roots music to convey this authenticity in a way that "breaks down the fourth wall," in reference to the invisible barrier between performer/performance and the audience. Thus, Finnan's observation is analogous to both narrative transport and personal resonance. "Part of the work for the artist, whether they call themselves a folk singer, singer-songwriter, or an Americana artist, is to observe and reflect. To share, and I think that's one of the distinguishing features [of roots music]. . . . I need to have the narrative of a story prescribed to me in a way that I can feel like I'm watching a movie" (pers. interview, May 18, 2021). As an illustration, Finnan references Jason Isbell's "Cumberland Gap" (2017) and Tracy Chapman's "Fast Car" (1988) as "windows into humanity."

Mary Muse, executive director of the Kerrville Folk Festival, further addresses the power of authenticity. "The center of our mission [the Kerrville Folk Festival] is about songwriting and the songwriting craft, and in so many ways you would say that has nothing to do with the social consciousness or social commentary. However, the best songs most often paint a picture in the first person and illuminate an experience, and even if it's not an experience that you have had, it makes it relatable. . . . The place where they [songwriters] wrote from is theirs and it's unique to them. Yet what makes the song powerful is that they're taking that very unique perspective and

Eliza Gilkyson at the Kerrville Folk Festival in Kerrville, Texas, on June 1, 2011. Courtesy Neale Eckstein.

giving it to you as well, and giving you the space to sit in there with them" (pers. interview, March 23, 2021).

Muse notes that the New Folk competition at the Kerrville Folk Festival has celebrated a multitude of songwriters that found ways to tell their stories and influence the greater social consciousness. Several of these songwriters, such as Slaid Cleaves, Steve Earle, Nanci Griffith, Robert Earl Keen, Lyle Lovett, and James McMurtry, have become prominent in the greater Americana culture. Notably, several of the artists included in this research have been judges, finalists, and/or winners in Kerrville.[13] To that end, the Kerrville Folk Festival community speaks to the larger Americana culture; and when asked to characterize the audience, Muse emphatically states, "Most of the people are very authentic and self-aware" (pers. interview, March 23, 2021).

Smart People

A largely authentic, self-aware audience likely leaves "faking it" as an unavailable option for Americana artists. Moreover, this community may not be satisfied with cursory storytelling. As Muse describes of the Kerrville audience, "They don't live life skimming the surface" (pers. interview, March 23, 2021). Colin Gilmore similarly describes the Americana audience as "thinking deeper" (pers. interview, December 21, 2021).

The same can be said for artists' perception of their audiences, which they see as very socially aware and bright. For example, T. Bone Burnett once said of Rodney Crowell, "Oh Rodney, I get it. You don't want to be rich. You play to the A students" (Shanahan 2017). That notion might broadly apply to Americana artists as well as what their fan bases perceive and expect of them.

Social awareness is often associated with education (e.g., Althaus 2003; Delli Carpini and Keeter 1996; Hayes and Lawless 2015). Indeed, the link between this culture and political tolerance is addressed above, and research points to a positive relationship between education and political tolerance (e.g., Stouffer 1955). The artists interviewed for this research generally accept that their audiences can detect straying from their "authentic selves."

Irakli Gabriel, who studied political science in college, states that perhaps the best way to characterize a given individual attending Anana Kaye performances is as "maybe someone that needs to think a bit more deeply" (pers. interview, February 12, 2021). When asked whether she recognizes her music as appealing to a highly intellectual crowd, Gilkyson accepts that reality. "I know. It really has limited my whole thing, but I had to make decisions about that and also what I do best. You know, what do I do that's me. Every time I've ever tried to compromise what I do, I suck at it, and I'm much better off being true to myself" (pers. interview, April 8, 2021). This remark marries the authenticity roots music audiences are seeking with artists' awareness of the general nature of their audiences and the culture.

Darrell Scott similarly explains that while the music often evokes downhome and/or blue-collar sentiments, the artists and audiences are sophisticated (pers. interview, April 21, 2021). Indeed, that is the impression conveyed by the entirety of artists interviewed. Scott is clear that this degree of social awareness is not necessarily synonymous with a high degree of formal education. However, it does not preclude the highly educated. On his audience's reception of the messages in his music, Scott says, "I have an intention to tell my truth and that it would connect with someone else. . . . From what I can tell, they're listening." Scott finds his audience, as well as other artists in the Americana musical space, bright and contemplative. He's hopeful that "there's more than just entertainment." Similarly, Rodney Crowell characterizes his audience as having a high degree of contemplation rather than formal education, and Rod Picott considers his audience "very literate" (Crowell pers. interview, March 3, 2021; Picott pers. interview, April 12, 2021).

Scott is quite reasoned in his characterization of his fan base, and the Americana audience more broadly. He explains that because the space is "small" relative to more commercial forms of music, the audience has to have a level of wherewithal to be aware of the artists and to locate venues for live performances. "You have to seek to it out. . . . It's like a really good restaurant." Scott further contends that if the authenticity and quality of the musical product remains impressive, "I'm fine with Americana being a well-kept secret. Maybe this allows the music to stay more pure" (pers. interview, April 21, 2021). Jon Bernstein's perception of Americana as a genre is that it has grown more viable as a commercial format in the last approximately ten years even if it's not as lucrative as other formats (pers. interview, March 17, 2021).

Like Scott, Slaid Cleaves sees his audiences as introspective and observant: "I'm very proud of my audience" (pers. interview, February 24, 2021). Cleaves, however, sees formal education as pervasive in his audience and speculates that the majority of his fan base is college educated.

"Getting It" and Elitism

While intelligence and social awareness do not necessarily convey elitism, this sentiment was nevertheless an undercurrent of much of the interviewing process. Application of "elitism" conveys negativity, but one should be cautious in that interpretation.

BettySoo provides an apt illustration about the negative side of elitism. When asked about how the audience would define Americana music, she reports that she has heard fans describe Americana as "Country music that doesn't suck" (pers. interview, September 21, 2021). Robbie Fulks appears to address this sentiment directly through humor in "Countrier than Thou" (2006): "He loved Bluegrass, Oh Brother. When I said Shania he sneered. 'That's a word I wouldn't utter. We like to keep it down-home up here."

Darrell Scott at Perth Concert Hall, taken on July 29, 2018. Courtesy Stefan Sobell.

While BettySoo understands that the "country music that doesn't suck" characterization comes from a place of appreciation for the music, she takes issue with the definition: "That is like erasing all of Black music. Not that there are no Black country artists, but the implication is a lot of times that it's [a] Rodney Crowell-Emmylou [Harris] country movement, the Gram Parsons kind of country movement—which is all stuff that I love and is the foundation for my music—but the implication is that it all comes from that. And then as an afterthought, 'oops, but we don't want to exclude people of color'" (pers. interview, September 21, 2021).

Kimbrough's aforementioned "My Right Wing Friend" (2020) also specifically addresses elitism lyrically. "And I know that I'm above you. I will always ever love you still, my right wing friend." Kimbrough explains that the song reflects not only one's perception that they are right, but also that divisiveness playing out on social media platforms stokes the intensity of differences (pers. interview, November 9, 2021).[14]

A more positive interpretation of elitism in this culture persists, however. Darrell Scott's discussion of the insular nature of this community points to the ability of artists and their fan bases to have an element of control that might not exist in more popular music (pers. interview, April 21, 2021). Scott explains that audiences may be uncomfortable with musical and lyrical experimentation at times, but the culture embraces both musical ambiguity and purity. "Uncomfortable is a real good place to be as an artist. [It's good to] have them [audiences] look at things in different ways."

Nostalgic and Hopeful

"There are these two people. Those that are hopeful for tomorrow and those that are nostalgic about yesterday," Todd Snider reflects (pers. interview, May 21, 2021). In political science we would often consider these groups as not often occupying the same space. For instance, Hetherington and Weiler's (2018) *Pickup or Prius* proffers that differing worldviews explain Americans' inability to converge on political and social issues. Fixed and nostalgic occupies the opposite pole of fluid and open to change. While Hetherington and Weiler (2018) discuss varied points on this scale they term mixed, the poles nevertheless mirror Snider's sentiment.

Americana culture is intrinsically linked to roots music, which is, by definition, rooted in the past. Tim O'Brien's appreciation for the history of bluegrass music and standards for which origins and authors have long been lost to time as well as his appreciation for American history from Thomas Jefferson to John Lewis, Joel Rafael's experiences in the counterculture and civil rights movement, which still influence his work, Reggie Harris's work on the Underground Railroad series and related educational programs, and the Drive-By Truckers' storytelling that addresses historical figures, such as Buford Pusser and Ramon Casiano, all signal an appreciation for and desire to learn from history.[15] Further, the frequent (though by no means ever-present) tendency for music in this space to be stripped down in terms of instrumentation and production also speaks to a continual embracing of roots and nostalgia.

Notably, the community extends beyond the artists and their proclivities. The Americana/roots music audience is small when compared to forms of contemporary music, but artists still need fan bases to support their work in order to survive solely on their art. The fan base loyalty that artists, journalists, and festival organizers/nonprofit executive directors report suggests that the audiences may be small, but they are sufficient to sustain a living.[16]

In turn, audiences evidently embrace this music, which often can be characterized as nostalgic.

Alternatively, political tolerance and progressive political attitudes permeate this culture. Hopefulness and the desire to create, rather than recreate, a more diverse and inclusive society is characteristic of those occupying this musical space. Lucinda Williams's "World Without Tears" (2003) provides an illustration of bleakness meeting hope. "If we lived in a world without tears, how would heartbeats know when to stop? How would blood know which body to flow outside of? How would bullets find the guns?" Without specifically addressing contemporary politics, struggle and strife associated with agriculture, region, alcohol, etc., Williams is able to evoke the same despair while still inspiring hope. Such raw emotion mixed with hope can also be seen to a degree in folksinger Tracy Chapman's "Fast Car" (1988), which infiltrated popular music before the establishment of the Americana charts. "You got a fast car. I got a plan to get us out of here. I been working at the convenience store. Managed to save a little bit of money. Won't have to drive too far. Just 'cross the border and into the city. You and I can both get jobs and finally see what it means to be living."

Aengus Finnan's approach to serving Folk Alliance International is an appropriate illustration of how the Americana culture manages to occupy poles. Finnan's appreciation for Canadian and Irish musical roots is evident. He speaks of his playing traditional Irish songs in Irish bars in Canada before being able to play his own songs and his friends' songs. He understands the roots music culture from the perspective of the person in the crowd, on the farm, in the office organizing, and on stage performing. Finnan's explanation for his vision for FAI was rooted in the past by a desire to recognize and include indigenous musics as well as urban-inspired music and the music shared by the Americana troubadours. Thus, Finnan's mission is to look backward in order to create a more inclusive future for the many faces of the "common man." The Americana culture similarly embraces roots and looks backward while pushing an inclusive and diverse narrative forward.

Summary

Shovels and Rope's "St. Anne's Parade" reflects the hopeful narrative of marrying nostalgia and progress.[17] In reference to the Mardi Gras parade sponsored by the Société de Saint Anne, which began marching in 1969 (see Knapp 2012), Cary Ann Hearst and Michael Trent sing of community, personal history, and celebration. "They canceled a parade or two for weather. The kings and saints, their robes all soaking wet. But we were happy just to all be there together. Stoned on the porch, smoking all Nikki's cigarettes. We've been riding down this highway now for all these years. Breathing in the dust along the way. But it's the kindness of a friend that is remembered in the end. It is a debt that is a pleasure to repay."

Despite Americana's hopeful narrative, the Americana culture reflects some of the stereotypes it seeks to challenge. This chapter sought to provide a sketch of the Americana audience and broader culture. Clear trends emerged. First, this audience is older. Rarely do artists see their fan bases as younger than forty, and many see fifty as a more accurate low age. Second, this audience is overwhelmingly white despite the culture seeking to promote diversity and inclusion. Third, this group is smart. While the music and the culture appeal to a blue-collar sensibility, the audience is socially aware and often highly educated. Fourth, elitist may be an appropriate label for individuals in this culture.

Care should be taken when applying "elitist," however. This is not necessarily a normative assessment, and the term is intended to signify an appreciation of/desire for "small" and "high quality," not "better than." Brandi Carlile's post to social media platform Instagram about her song "Right on Time" (2021) being moved from Grammy consideration in the American Roots genre to Pop illustrates the extent to which artists and the Americana culture embrace being "smaller" and outside of the mainstream (see Mier 2021): "While I am flattered to be considered 'pop' as a 40 year old crooning lesbian mother, I'd be lying if I said I wasn't a bit surprised and disappointed to learn the Recording Academy decided to move 'Right On Time' out of the American Roots genre and into the pop category. Being recognized by the Grammys—in any form—is a great honor. I just want folks to know that this wasn't my decision. Regardless, it doesn't change who I am or what my Americana community means to me."

Finally, rather than fitting nicely into nostalgic or hopeful attitude camps, this culture embraces both. As established in the preceding chapters, diversity is encouraged. The roots music culture is generally inclusive, the lyrical messaging often imparts diversity, and the growing professional infrastructure in the form of Americana charts and awards specifically seeks to honor and include racial/ethnic minority artists. Nevertheless, the rub with the insular nature of the culture and related elitism is the inability of these messages of diversity and inclusion to reach unfamiliar listeners.

One has to ask, however, if this becomes a circular argument. More specifically, if this music and messaging were more widely disseminated, would the comfort of the community and the potency of the messaging be lost? To that end, the following chapter tests the impact of exposure to Americana music on largely unfamiliar listeners.

5
THE IMPACT

Amythyst Kiah, an African American lesbian, tackles a myriad of stereotypes relating to race, sexual orientation, and even roots music itself in "Black Myself" (2021). In a 2021 *New York Times* interview, Kiah reported some challenges with initially attempting to force herself into the confines of a specific genre, but she underscores that she has always been drawn to a variety of musical influences (Hight 2021). Certainly "Black Myself," which was released on the Americana-focused Rounder label and earned both a Grammy nomination for Best American Roots Song and a nomination by the Americana Music Association for Song of the Year in 2021, poignantly embraces cultural and musical diversity. "I don't pass the test of the paper bag 'cause I'm Black myself. I pick the banjo up and they sneer at me 'cause I'm Black Myself . . . I want to sweep that gal right off her feet, but I'm Black Myself. I'm tired of walking 'round with no shoes on, but I'm Black Myself. And your precious God ain't gonna bless me 'cause I'm Black Myself."

The preceding chapters have touched on the origins of the Americana format—broadly conceived, stereotypical sketches of artists, thematic lyrical content, artists' assessments of their music and audiences, and the culture that serves as a vehicle for narrative transport. A concise, yet informative summary of the preceding chapters can then be distilled to the following points:

1. Americana's musical roots are within and across several constituent genres that have diverse regional, cultural, and racial origins; Cultural stereotypes with one foot in the decades-old counterculture view of

folk music and the other foot firmly rooted in variations of the cowboy permeate Americana;

2. While all Americana music certainly could not be termed "partisan" or "political," this culture generally takes on a progressive and/or socially aware message overtly through lyrics and/or more subtly through venues and community interaction;
3. The Americana culture and audience can be described as possessing high levels of political tolerance and group empathy;
4. Stereotypes serve to insulate the genre from more diverse audiences; and
5. Stereotypes may also serve to deliver a message of inclusivity to previously message-resistant audiences.

This chapter begins to explore this final point by describing the manner of testing the relationship between exposure to music that can be characterized as Americana and political attitudes with an experimental design similar to that used by Bonnette (2015). Bonnette's primary focus is the impact of political rap music on Black political attitudes, while this research considers the impact of Americana exposure on both white and non-white political attitudes. In turn, I first specify testable hypotheses before addressing the sample descriptive statistics below. I then explain each of the eight experimental manipulations before summarizing the virtues of the sample and experimental design. Afterward, I turn to the empirical results.

General Hypotheses

The theoretical development and lyrical analyses presented in the previous chapters lead to the expectation that exposure to Americana music may impact political attitudes relating to demographic diversity (i.e., race, ethnicity, sexual orientation). Specifically, I expect that the dissonance associated with an unfamiliar medium will result in respondents' greater willingness to consider the message, ultimately resulting in more favorable evaluations of minority group members. This may be seen in evaluations of policies seen as racially coded, such as welfare (see for example Gilens 1999) and crime/policing (see for example Peffley and Hurwitz 2010), as well as punitive measures (e.g., Chiricos, Welch, and Gertz 2004; Fording, Soss, and Schram 2011). It may also be seen in evaluations of immigrants and the LGBTQ+ community. In turn, I expect exposure to Americana music, which is not widely disseminated and may be erroneously linked to antiegalitarian political attitudes, to result in less support for such policies or diminished agreement with antiminority attitudes.

Sample

In order to test the relationship between exposure to music associated with the Americana culture and political attitudes, I utilize a survey-based experiment administered to college students in 2021 in two waves via a Qualtrics link.[1] The first wave was administered predominately to students at Valdosta State University and Lewis University.[2] The second wave was administered to students at both Valdosta State University and Tennessee Technological University approximately two months after the survey closed for the first wave.[3] A total of 384 respondents completed the survey. The first wave unsurprisingly supplied a larger portion of the respondents (approximately 90 percent of the total). This is expected, given that university enrollment is significantly greater in the fall and spring terms compared to the summer.[4] For instance, 11,231 students were enrolled in Valdosta State University in the spring of 2021, while only 6,151 students were enrolled across 2021 summer terms.[5] Students in both waves were recruited primarily from courses required of all students rather than classes associated solely with specific majors.[6]

The previous chapters established the Americana community as overwhelmingly white and over forty. The sample utilized in this research, however, is overwhelmingly young (approximately 70 percent are traditional college age, eighteen to twenty-two years old), and greater than 28 percent of respondents identify as African American. Moreover, nearly 12 percent of respondents combined identify as Latinx, Asian/Pacific Islander, Native American, or "Other." More than 79 percent of respondents are thirty years old or younger, and approximately 89 percent of the sample is under the age of forty. In terms of age and race, this convenience sample could be seen as the antithesis of the Americana community.

The sample similarly does not mirror the Americana community in terms of sex or sexual orientation.[7] There is a very large nonheterosexual population (including those respondents identifying as bisexual, homosexual, and the two transgendered respondents that indicated they most closely identified with transgender in comparison to other options) that exceeds 20 percent. This group is predominately women, with fifty-nine female respondents identifying as nonheterosexual, compared to eighteen male respondents identifying as such, however. Heterosexual women are the modal group, with 214 respondents, constituting greater than 56 percent of the sample. The crosstabulation below presents the joint distribution of sex and sexual orientation.

Table 5.1. Sex/Sexual Orientation Distribution

	Sexual Orientation		
Biological Sex	***Heterosexual***	***Non-Heterosexual***	***Total***
Male	90	18	108
Female	214	59	273
Total	304	77	381

Respondents identifying as Protestant Christians are the largest religious group in the sample at greater than 60 percent.[8] Respondents identifying as non-religious (either Agnostic or Atheist) make up the second largest religious/irreligious group in the sample at 16.28 percent. Christians, however, constitute nearly 70 percent of the sample when Catholic-identifying students are combined with Protestants. Notably, the sample includes no Jewish respondents, only three Muslim respondents, one Hindu respondent, and five Buddhists respondents. Interestingly, nearly 12 percent of the sample identifies as religious "Other" (which should not be confused with religious "None"), while the comparable national statistic would place "other faiths" and "other world religions" combined at less than 2 percent of Americans (Pew Research Center 2015). This discrepancy may seem surprising, but recent research points to growth in those Americans claiming to be "Spiritual but not Religious" (SBNR) (see Hertzke, Olson, den Dulk, and Fowler 2018; McCarthy, Olson, and Garrand 2019). Additionally, the 16.28

percent of this sample identifying as "None (Atheist/Agnostic)" is considerably less than the comparable national statistics, which suggest that nearly 23 percent of Americans identify as religious "Nones," including those that identify as "Atheist," "Agnostic," and "Nothing in Particular" (Pew Research Center 2015). More than a third of this group is under the age of thirty, and the median age of the religiously unaffiliated has dropped to a low of 36 percent.

Chart 5.1 presents the religious identification breakdown of the sample. "All Christians" is included in the chart although respondents were not presented this option. Rather, this simple combination of "Protestant Christian" and "Catholic" is included in order to demonstrate the dominance of affiliation with Christian denominations across respondents. Notably, despite the rise in religious "nones," seven out of ten Americans continue to identify as Christian (Pew 2015). Thus, the preponderance of Christian-identifying respondents in this sample (69.51 percent) mirrors that in the greater American population.[9]

Given that negative views of homosexuality are often associated with expressing more literal interpretations of the Bible (see Barth, Overby, and Huffmon 2009; Whitehead 2014) and that this research specifically consid-

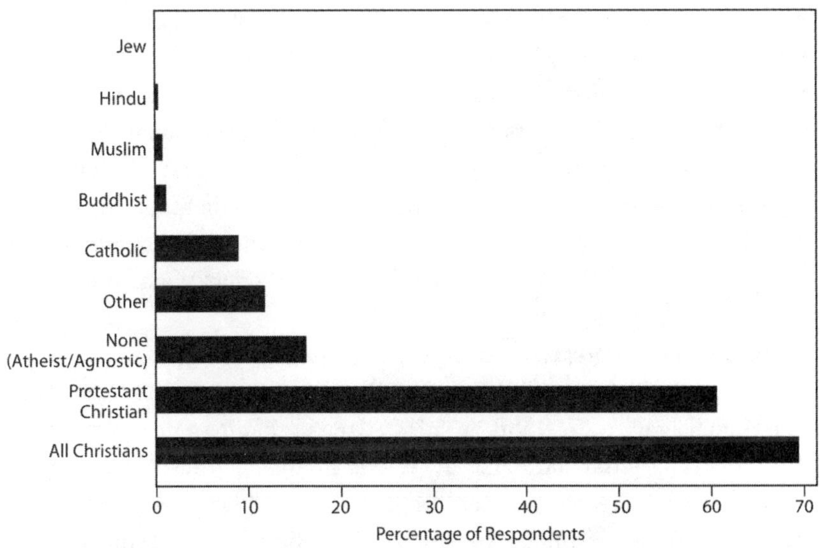

Chart 5.1. Religious Identification

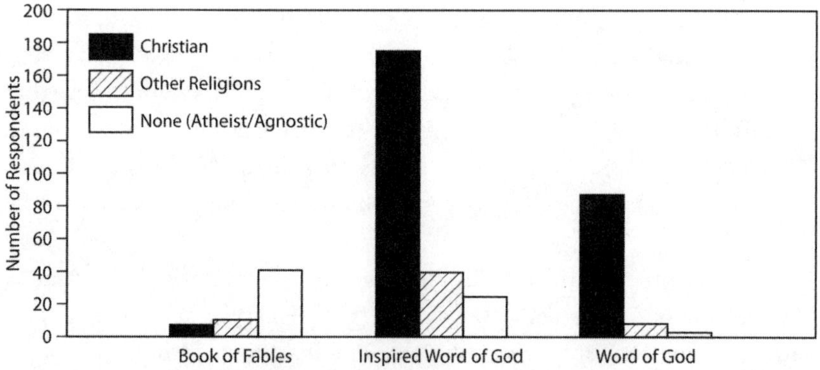

Chart 5.2. Biblical Literalism

ers attitudes toward diversity and inclusion in the Americana community, a consideration of biblical literalism is important.[10] Biblical literalism is measured on a crude three-point ordinal scale from (1) "The Bible is a book of fables created by men" to (3) "The Bible is the actual Word of God. It is to be taken literally." The midpoint on the scale, "The Bible is the inspired Word of God, but not everything in it is to be taken literally, word for word," is the mode, with 236 respondents (61.98 percent) selecting this response. Interestingly, this is also the modal response for those identifying with religions other than Christianity (i.e., Jews, Muslims, Buddhists, Hindus, Others) as well as approximately 37 percent of those reporting a lack of religiosity (i.e., "None [Atheist/Agnostic]"). Chart 5.2 illustrates attitudes toward the Bible.

Utilizing college students as a sample may offer conventional challenges, such as the "college sophomore problem," but they also offer a unique population that is typically less likely to have experiences that those with more crystalized opinions possess and they are in a gray area between not educated and educated.[11] Nevertheless, one's parental educational attainment speaks to social background.

Respondents were asked to indicate the highest level of education attained by their parents/guardians. Available responses range from "Less than High School" to "MD and/or PhD."[12] Greater than 70 percent of respondents report parents/guardians having a minimum of an associate's degree. And 44 percent of respondents report parents/guardians having a minimum of a bachelor's degree. Impressively, more than one-quarter of the sample reports parents/guardians as possessing an advanced degree (e.g., MA, MBA, JD, DVM, DDS, DMD, MD, PhD).[13]

The sample skews Democratic in partisan affiliation and liberal in ideological identity. However, these measures are not perfectly correlated (.74). Party identification is measured on a six-point ordinal scale from "Strong Democrat" (1) to "Strong Republican" (6). The midpoint of the scales was purposely excluded to encourage unaffiliated respondents to choose between the major parties. A similar approach was utilized with ideology by excluding "moderate" and creating a six-point scale from "Strong Liberal" (1) to "Strong Conservative" (6).[14] Mid-points may serve as a means to opt out of expressing true preferences. Thus, eliminating the middle position may encourage true responses, while those who honestly identify as "Moderate" or "Neither Republican Nor Democratic" would presumably skip these questions.

While nearly 68 percent and 63 percent of the sample identifies as Democratic and liberal in varying degrees, the modal categories were not extremes. Greater than half of the sample identifies as "Democrat," and greater than 46 percent identifies as liberal. Notably, nearly 31 percent of the sample identifies as weak partisans, and approximately one-third of respondents identify as weak ideologues (precisely equal divisions of Weak Liberal and Weak Conservative identifiers).

The survey was administered following a highly polarized presidential election. Despite greater than 19 percent of the sample reporting either not voting or being ineligible to vote in the 2020 presidential election, approximately 21 percent of respondents indicate having voted for the then-incumbent president, Republican Donald Trump.[15] Greater than 54 percent of respondents indicate having voted for the eventual winner, Democrat Joseph Biden. Less than 5 percent of respondents reported voting for a candidate other than Trump or Biden.

Because social media use has become pervasive in American culture and because research suggests widely disseminated information gleaned from social media is both subject to inaccuracies (e.g., Flynn, Nyhan, and Reifler 2017) and consumers often believe the false information (e.g., Allcott and Gentzkow 2017), understanding that greater than 40 percent of the sample identifies social media as their primary source of political information is key. Allcott and Gentzkow (2017, 2011) illustrate the concern with acquiring political information via social media: "Content can be relayed among users with no significant third party filtering, fact-checking, or editorial judgment."

This, too, likely distinguishes the sample from the Americana audience. Given age and level of social awareness, one could anticipate that this audience is more likely to acquire political news via social media. For example, while YouTube and Facebook are widely used across age ranges in the United States, other social media platforms such as SnapChat, Instagram, Tiktok, and Twitter are used less by middle-aged and older Americans than those thirty and younger (Auxier and Anderson 2021). Further, Americans ages eighteen to twenty-nine make up the largest age cohort of users in each of these platforms with the exception of Facebook. Therefore, while the survey utilized in this sample did not ask respondents to indicate their social media platform preference(s), respondents' patterns of use are likely very distinct from the Americana audience.

Sample parameters suggest this sample is very distinct from the Americana community in many key demographic areas. Specifically, the sample is dramatically young, racially diverse, diverse in terms of sexual orientation, female-dominated, and avid social media users, while the Americana community at the most relaxed low age range is a minimum of forty years old, predominately white, majority male, and generally lacking diversity in sexual orientation despite a propensity to espouse tolerance, empathy, and diversity. On the other hand, there is some overlap between the sample and the Americana community in the form of preponderance of left-leaning ideology and Democratic partisan identification.

Despite the similarities in partisanship and ideological predispositions, this sample is unlikely to have a high degree of exposure to music associated with the Americana culture.

Experimental Design

An experimental manipulation was embedded in the survey following a short series of questions about general political attitudes and voting choice.[16] This manipulation involved the presentation of an audio file containing one of eight songs as explained below.[17] Measures serving as dependent variables followed the application of these stimuli, which were administered proportionally through the Qualtrics platform, assuring that approximately the same number of respondents received each treatment. Participants were randomly assigned to one of eight treatments before being asked about the music and additional political attitudes, such as attitudes toward policies associated with specific minority groups (e.g., gay marriage).[18] These treatments vary the musical format (i.e., Americana-folk, Americana-rhythm and blues, commercial country, and rap) and exposure to/avoidance of lyrical racial messaging. Care was taken to ensure that the two songs in a given genre were performed by the same artist to minimize extraneous variables (e.g., female versus male voices, more popular versus less popular artists).

Because roots music is so varied, the four Americana treatments were necessary. To this end, two treatments by the same artist can be characterized as Americana in the rhythm and blues tradition while two by another artist can best be labeled folk.[19] Respondents were not exposed to video and/or images, leaving treatments as only audio with a distinctly male lead voice. This approach ensures that elements such as perception of artist gender, attractiveness, venue aesthetics, video quality, etc., did not interfere with consumption and message resonance. Each treatment is addressed below.

Importantly, only two constituent genres of the Americana format (i.e., folk, rhythm and blues) are included in the statistical analyses provided in this research. While analyses of other constituent genres would be useful to this and similar research, their inclusion would have served to create additional experimental treatments, which would have decreased the number of observations within each cell. Therefore, I selected folk and rhythm and blues because the former presents a clear connection to one of the prevailing stereotypes addressed in previous chapters and the latter, while not commercial country, has lyrical elements that fit into country music and presents a juxtaposition with the acoustic delivery of folk.

Similarly, African Americans are the most obvious minority group addressed in the applicable experimental treatments. Certainly one could argue that the inclusion of treatments explicitly addressing immigrants, the LGBTQ+ community, etc., would be beneficial. Their inclusion would have also further reduced the number of observations within each treatment. Moreover, extant research implies the activation of considerations about a given minority group prime intersectionality considerations of other minority groups (e.g., Moreau, Nuno-Perez, and Sanchez 2019). Therefore, the approach employed here is both appropriate and understandable.

Commercial Country Addressing Race

Commercial country musician Eric Church released "Stick That in Your Country Song" in 2020 on an album with the same title. The song, however, was not written by Church.[20] Church subsequently received a 2021 Grammy nomination for Best Country Solo Performance for the song.

"Stick That in Your Country Song" does not explicitly state "race" and/or "African American"; however, the racial undertones of the first two verses are clear through references to Detroit, which is overwhelmingly majority African American, and urban Baltimore.[21] "Stick That in Your Country Song" begins, "Take me on up to Detroit City. Jails are full, the factories empty. Momma's crying, young boys dying. Under that red, white, and blue still flying. Drop me off in Baltimore. Where every window has a plywood board. Where dreams become drugs and guns. The only way out is to shoot or run."

Race Neutral Commercial Country

Church is one of the songwriters for the second commercial country song used in this analysis. "Springsteen" was released on Church's 2012 *Chief* album.[22] While Bruce Springsteen, the titular character in the song, has made political statements, written politically charged music, performed for/endorsed political candidates, and even authored a book with former Democratic president Barack Obama, this song lacks political messaging entirely.[23] Further, those sampled are unlikely to have a depth of awareness of Springsteen's history, given their age.

Rap Addressing Race

Race is a core element of rap music, which is reflective of hip-hop culture. In turn, finding a rap song addressing race was not difficult. J. Cole is a Grammy Award-winning rapper and songwriter. "Folgers Crystals" from Cole's 2015 *Revenge of the Dreamers II* album is the rap treatment addressing race.[24] This song contains a myriad of references to race, including stating "nigga" thirteen times and the lyric "They see a Black man shine, first thing they do is throw their shade."

Race Neutral Rap

The inclusion of J. Cole's work was selected for the ability to locate a rap song that did not directly reference or imply race as well as his general prominence in hip-hop culture. Utilizing "Folgers Crystals" requires utilizing another rap song by J. Cole. To this end, Cole's "The Plan" (2021) is the rap treatment that does not address race.

Americana-Folk Addressing Race

Todd Snider released "The Devil You Know" on his 2006 album with the same title. The album version of the song verges on rhythm and blues, but an acoustic version of the song is utilized as a treatment in this research. This version reflects Snider's more typical folk delivery. "The Devil You Know" addresses race with lyrics such as the following:

1. "Helicopters over the house again. We got the projects two or three blocks from here. They pull these kids over for Driving-While-African and the ones with the warrants always run in fear";
2. "This poor kid probably never had a chance to give a fuck. He wouldn't know good luck from a debutante. He's got to find a way to be Steve McNair or Young Buck or he's just tough luck looking for a prison to haunt";
3. "I wouldn't trade that for my crooked hat. Or my gang or my gun or my waist full of pagers. For a job deep-frying shit for richer teenagers. If that's where it's at and no one's gonna help, how you gonna blame a man for helping himself? There's war going on and the poor can't win"; and
4. "All the white people talking about the hope and the light. There ain't no hope in Sam Levy, just guns and drugs. We ain't building bridges, we're just training thugs."

Race Neutral Americana-Folk

The inclusion of "The Devil You Know" necessitates the use of another song performed by Todd Snider for the Americana-Folk variant that does not include racial references. I chose "Too Soon to Tell" from Snider's 2012 *Agnostic Hymns and Stoner Fables* album.

Americana-Rhythm and Blues Addressing Race

Jason Isbell and the 400 Unit's 2017 "White Man's World" is a very clear statement on white male privilege. The song, found on the Grammy Award-winning *The Nashville Sound,* features a full band and electric guitar in contrast to the stripped-down version of "The Devil You Know" utilized as an experimental treatment in this research. Moss (2017) of *Rolling Stone* says the following of "White Man's World": "Isbell comes to terms with the world in which he thrives: one that sees women like his wife slighted, people of color targeted by police." Lyrics include "I'm a white man living on a white man's street. I've got the bones of the red man under my feet. The highway runs through their burial grounds. Past the oceans of cotton," and "I'm a white man looking in a Black man's eyes. Wishing I'd never been one of the guys. Who pretended not to hear another white man's joke. Oh, the times ain't forgotten." "White Man's World" does not offer as many references specific to African Americans as "The Devil You Know"; however, race and gender are clearly the thematic foundation. Moreover, Isbell sings the lyrics addressing African Americans emphatically, and "oceans of cotton" very clearly reflects the historical role of enslaved African Americans as field hands in the southern United States.

Race Neutral Americana-Rhythm and Blues

"Super 8" (2013) by Jason Isbell, with the 400 Unit as the backing band, also presents a harder, rhythm and blues variant of Americana. This song doesn't address race, and has been described as "country-rock storytelling" in *Rolling Stone* (Hermes 2013).[25]

Importantly, a consideration of lyrics may convey sentiments that can be connected to the broader societal and/or political environment. However, an analysis addressing music written by and/or regularly performed by the artist as opposed to contrived lyrics by a scientist to control the message is unlikely to produce clinically perfect treatments. Therefore, songs were selected in such a way that ensured race was only referenced in one song of two by the same artist and that overtly partisan and ideological references were absent.

Exposure to/Appreciation for Americana

Per expectations, few respondents recall exposure to Americana music prior to the application of the survey. Table 5.2 illustrates respondents' reactions to the respective treatments, including whether they had been exposed to the song and/or artist, whether they typically listened to music they perceive as in the same genre as the song they heard, and whether they enjoyed the music.

Despite four of eight manipulations falling beneath the broad Americana umbrella, only eleven participants across the four treatments report having been exposed to the artists and/or songs prior to the survey. Meanwhile, forty-two respondents report having been exposed to J. Cole and/or the rap songs presented, and thirty-one respondents report having been exposed to Eric Church and/or the commercial country songs presented. While exposure to Americana was expected to be less than country and rap, the dramatic difference is surprising given Jason Isbell's multiple Grammy nominations and numerous accolades.

Inquiring about preferred genre produced slightly different findings, with twenty-four respondents reporting typically listening to folk music (in varying degrees) and nineteen respondents reporting the same of Americana in the rhythm and blues vein. Alternatively, fifty respondents indicate typically listening to rap music, and twenty-eight respondents indicate the same of commercial country music. Perhaps the lack of familiarity explains both versions of Americana being less liked by participants compared to rap and commercial country. Regardless, this descriptive data underscores a general lack of familiarity with music associated with the Americana culture across respondents.

Table 5.2 provides another key illustration relating to the Americana treatments. Specifically, the race neutral treatment was better received than the racialized treatment when one considers commercial country or rap. The same cannot be said for Americana, where those exposed to the racialized folk treatment appear to have enjoyed the music (65.12 percent) more so than those presented with the race neutral treatment (56.25 percent). The

Table 5.2. Reaction to Treatments

Treatment	*Prior Exposure to Song/Artist#*	*Typically Listens to this Genre#**	*Enjoyed Music/ Song#**
Race Neutral Commercial Country	42.31% (22)	32.69% (17)	76.92% (40)
Racialized Commercial Country	18.37% (9)	22.45% (11)	55.10% (27)
Race Neutral Rap	44.90% (22)	51.02% (25)	75.51% (37)
Racialized Rap	38.46% (20)	48.08% (25)	69.23% (36)
Race Neutral Americana-Folk	12.50% (6)	27.08% (13)	56.25% (27)
Racialized Americana-Folk	2.33% (1)	26.19% (11)	65.12% (28)
Race Neutral Americana-Rhythm & Blues	5.74% (2)	21.28% (10)	40.43% (19)
Racialized Americana-Rhythm & Blues	3.77% (2)	16.98% (9)	50.94% (27)
Commercial Country (Both)	36.69% (31)	27.72% (28)	66.34% (67)
Rap (Both)	41.58% (42)	49.50% (50)	72.28% (73)
Americana-Folk (Both)	7.78% (7)	26.67% (24)	60.44% (55)
Americana-Rhythm & Blues (Both)	4.00% (4)	19% (19)	46.00% (46)

Raw frequencies in parentheses.

* Responses to these survey questions are based on a 6-point ordinal scale from Strongly Disagree to Strongly Agree. The percentage reported here is based on the combined responses "Somewhat Agree" (4), "Agree" (5), and "Strongly Agree" (6).

same can be said of the rhythm and blues treatments, where greater than half (50.94 percent) of those receiving the racialized treatment enjoyed the music while 40.43 percent of those receiving the race neutral rhythm and blues variant reported enjoying the song.

Importantly, all demographic data (including partisanship and ideology) were collected after exposure to a given experimental treatment and measures addressing attitudes toward minorities that are used as dependent variables.[26] Similarly, the questions assessing political attitudes key to this study were collected following exposure.

Design Summary

Bob Dylan's "Things Have Changed" was written for the film *Wonder Boys* and resulted in Dylan winning an Academy Award for Best Original Song.[27] Dylan stated, "I want to thank the members of the Academy who were bold enough to give me this award for this song which obviously [is] a song that doesn't pussyfoot around nor turn a blind eye to human nature," in his remote acceptance speech for the award.[28]

In terms of human nature as conveyed in the song, Dylan sings, "I've been walking forty miles of bad road. If the Bible is right, the world will explode. I've been trying to get as far away from myself as I can. Some things are too hot to touch. The human mind can only stand so much. You can't win with a losing hand." These lyrics speak to individuals' ability to process dissonant information, and could be seen as applying to minority groups' seeing the deck as stacked against them from the onset. Notably, homosexuality is an evident theme of *Wonder Boys.*

Bob Dylan has certainly spoken to stacked decks regarding racial issues throughout his career. Specifically in the cowritten 1976 "Hurricane," Dylan takes on racism and the justice system. "All of Rubin's cards were marked in advance. The trial was a pig-circus, he never had a chance. The judge made Rubin's witnesses drunkards from the slums. To the white folks who watched he was a revolutionary bum. And to the Black folks he was just a crazy nigger. No one doubted that he pulled the trigger. And though they could not produce the gun. The D.A. said he was the one that did the deed. And the all-white jury agreed."[29]

"Things Have Changed" and "The Hurricane" collectively illustrate the goal of the experimental design explicated in this chapter. Regarding the former, dissonance is a key to understanding the potential impact of Americana music on unfamiliar listeners, such as the respondents involved in this sample. Conceptions of "white" and "rural" as much as "hippie" and "cowboy" may fuel the unaware audience's expectations of the music from the initial moment of exposure. Regarding the latter, clearly tapping into racial injustice (or injustices faced by varied minorities in the United States) via lyrics is necessary to determining the potential impact of this music on attitudes regarding minority groups.

Empirical Analyses

Jason Isbell poignantly ends the 2016 Americana Music Association Song of the Year "24 Frames" with, "You thought God was an architect, now you know. He's sitting in a black car ready to go. You made some new friends after the show. But you'll forget their names. In 24 frames." The song can be uncomfortable, yet there's something about its evocation of family that nevertheless inspires hope: "And this is how you make yourself worthy of the love that she gave to you back when you didn't own a beautiful thing." The same can be said for Nathaniel Rateliff, who reminds, "Say the glass is clear, but all this fear. Starts a-leaving a mark. Your idle hands are all that stands. From your time in the dark. But it's still alright," in the title track of his 2020 album, which was nominated for Album of the Year by the Americana Music Association.[30]

Tackling difficult subject matter through music is at the core of this analysis. The experimental treatments elucidated above—and those manipulations that tackled race and diversity—may very well leave the listener facing a certain amount of dissonance and/or ambivalence. More specifically, one may enjoy the music and appreciate the narrative while understanding the dark themes. To that end, the remainder of this chapter considers the results of the experimental analyses.

Dependent Variables

Models use a given dependent variable designed to capture support for minorities and/or policies associated with minorities. Three variables address African Americans, while one represents immigrants broadly defined, and one explicitly addresses the LGBTQ+ community. Importantly, these measures do not directly ask about approval of minority groups so as not to activate respondent concerns about social desirability. In turn, more subtle measures are used.

Variables addressing African Americans require qualification, given that they are rooted in racially coded language (see Jamieson 1992). Peffley, Hurtwitz, and Sniderman (1997) provide an illustration of the connection between policy attitudes and racial coding. Specifically, they find whites' negative racial stereotypes prime evaluations of both welfare and crime. Gilens (1996, 1999) also evidences welfare as code for African American, while further research illustrates the connection between the impact of racial code words in relation to crime (e.g., Gilliam and Iyengar 2000; Peffley and Hurwitz 2004).

Based on the foregoing, the three variables used to assess attitudes toward African Americans indirectly ask about punishment, policing, and welfare recipients. Specifically, these variables state:

1. One good way to teach certain people right from wrong is to give them a good stiff punishment when they get out of line;
2. The police in this country can be trusted to treat everyone fairly and equally; and
3. Welfare recipients prefer to live off welfare rather than being self-supporting.

The two remaining dependent variables concern immigrants and the LGBTQ+ community. Regarding the former, race, ethnicity, nor country of origin are specified. Regarding the latter, respondents were asked about gay marriage rather than directly asking about level of support for/approval of the LGBTQ+ community more broadly defined. Nevertheless, these two variables address policy attitudes relating to immigrants and the LGBTQ+ community directly rather than subtly (as with the preceding dependent variables that utilize racially coded language) by specifying the following:

1. Legal immigrants mostly fill jobs that U.S. citizens do not want; and
2. Gay marriage should not be legal.[31]

Responses to each of the prompts used as dependent variables range from "Strongly Disagree" to "Strongly Agree" on a six-point scale. The middle position was excluded, forcing respondents to lean toward agreement or disagreement or skip the questions.

Model Specification

Because each of the eight treatments was randomly assigned to respondents, a myriad of controls is not necessary to determine the relationship between exposure to the stimuli and political attitudes. However, given the strong relationship between political attitudes and variables such as partisanship, sex, religion, news consumption, and social background characteristics, related controls are utilized in the models below. Notably, the correlation between affiliation with a Christian denomination (either Protestant or Catholic) and attitudes toward the Bible is unexpectedly relatively low (.47). Similarly, neither of these measures is highly correlated with religious attendance (Christian = .47; biblical literalism = .45). Resultantly, one cannot presume a single measure of religion is sufficient. In turn, all three are utilized in the model below. Likewise, parental education and parental income are not highly correlated (.40), resulting in the inclusion of both.

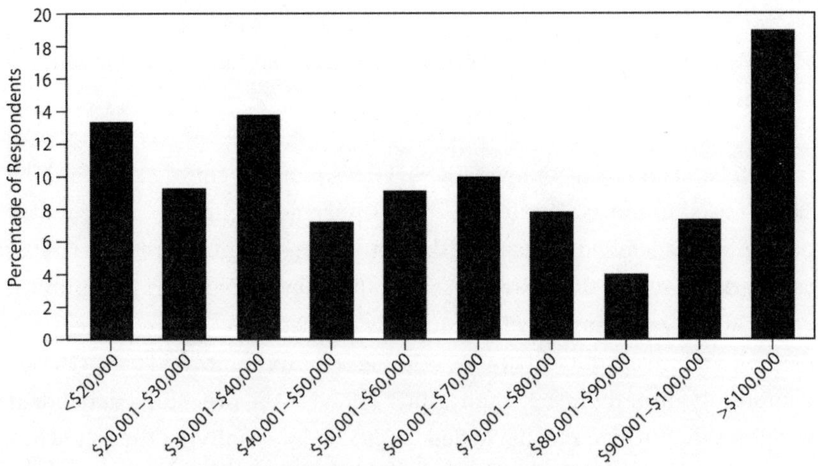

Graph 5.1. Parent/Guardian Reported Income (Reported as Percentage of Sample)

Similarly, the concerns with the widespread use of social media to glean political information addressed previously necessitate a control for political news consumption via these platforms. A dummy variable representing social media political news consumer is then included. Regardless of whether respondents gather political information via social media, television, professors, parents, etc., the preferred medium is not synonymous with the amount of political news consumed. Indeed, social media news consumer and political news consumption are not correlated in a meaningful way (.07). In turn, the following model includes the latter control as well.

> Attitude/Assessment = Treatment + Partisanship + Biblical Literalism + Christian + Religious Attendance + Parental Education + Parental Income + Social Media User + Political News Consumption + White + Male.[32]

Christian, white, and male as well as social media user and the key independent variable, treatment, are dummy variables. Treatment reflects one of the four Americana treatments and the corresponding commercial music treatments (e.g., folk addressing race versus commercial country addressing race). Importantly, parental education is simplified so that the highest value represents greater than a bachelor's degree rather than splitting hairs with advanced degree completion.[33]

Ordinary least squares regression models are utilized in the models below for ease of interpretation.

Experimental Results

The statistical analyses detailed below reflect results relating to seven of the eight experimental manipulations across eleven statistical models, and except for one model all conform to the expectations set forth in the hypotheses presented above.[34] Only one of the treatments, race neutral Americana-rhythm and blues versus race neutral commercial country, failed to produce any statistically significant results regarding exposure to the experimental treatment.[35] To this end, I speculate why this manipulation is different in the summary of this chapter as well as in the concluding chapter of this book.[36]

Race Neutral Americana-Folk versus Race Neutral Commercial Country:

Table 5.3. Americana-Folk Treatments vs. Contemporary Country (Race Neutral)

	Welfare Recipients Prefer to Live Off Welfare Rather than Being Self-Supporting	*Legal Immigrants Mostly Fill Jobs that U.S. Citizens Do Not Want*
Treatment	-.63*	.54*
	(.27)	(.27)
Party Identification (6=Republican)	.33**	-.13
	(.12)	(.13)
Biblical Literalism (3=Literal Word of God)	.02	.14
	(.28)	(.28)
Christian	-.31	.24
	(.39)	(.39)
Religious Attendance (5=>Once/Week)	.27*	.18
	(.13)	(.13)
Parental Education	.10	-.15
	(.12)	(.20)
Parental Income	-.03	-.05
	(.06)	(.06)
Social Media News User	.03	.00
	(.29)	(.29)
Political News Consumption	-.13	.06
	(.08)	(.08)
White	-.01	-.08
	(.36)	(.37)
Male	.12	-.78**
	(.29)	(.29)
R^2	.27	.27
n	89	90

OLS regression with robust standard errors in parentheses.

DV= Responses indicate agreement on a 7-point scale. 1= Strongly Disagree, 6=Strongly Agree

*** $p<0.001$, ** $p<0.01$, * $p<0.05$, † $p<0.1$

Table 5.3 illustrates the comparisons between exposure to Americana music in the folk tradition or commercial country music with neither directly addressing race. These results address attitudes toward welfare and attitudes toward legal immigrants' taking jobs that American citizens do not want. These findings indicate that respondents receiving the race neutral Americana-folk treatment as opposed to those exposed to the commercial country treatment that similarly does not address race are less likely to think that welfare recipients prefer to live off welfare rather than being self-supporting.

These findings further underscore a propensity toward diversity, as they indicate those receiving the race neutral Americana-folk manipulation are also more likely to think legal immigrants fill jobs US citizens do not want than are those receiving the race neutral commercial country manipulation. Implicitly, this means that those respondents receiving the folk-based treatment without references to race are less likely to think that legal immigrants are "stealing" jobs US citizens wish to have compared to the commercial country treatment that does not address race.

Racialized Americana-Folk versus Racialized Commercial Country: Table 5.4 presents findings regarding the comparison of folk music and commercial country music with racial themes to attitudes relating to punishment generally and gay marriage specifically. In particular, those respondents receiving the racialized Americana-folk treatment were less likely to agree that a good way to teach "certain people" right from wrong is by giving them a good stiff punishment when they get out of line than were those receiving the racialized commercial country manipulation. This finding achieves statistical significance at the less stringent .1 level, however.[37]

Table 5.4 likewise reveals an inverse relationship between opposition to gay marriage and exposure to Americana-folk with racial themes as opposed to exposure to racialized contemporary country music. In this case, respondents receiving the folk treatment were less likely to agree that gay marriage should not be legal compared to respondents receiving the racially themed commercial country music treatment. This relationship achieves statistical significance at the more conventional .05 level.

Race Neutral Americana-Folk versus Race Neutral Rap: Table 5.5 presents the lone instance in which exposure to one of the experimental manipulations impacted attitudes toward the police treating everyone equally

Table 5.4. Americana-Folk Treatments vs. Contemporary Country (Racial Reference)

	Teach "Certain People" Right from Wrong with a "Good Stiff Punishment"	*Gay Marriage Should Not Be Legal*
Treatment	-.42† (.24)	-.68* (.34)
Party Identification (6=Republican)	.04 (.11)	.16 (.15)
Biblical Literalism (3=Literal Word of God)	.85*** (.24)	.69* (.34)
Christian	-.95‡ (.37)	-.18 (.52)
Religious Attendance (5=>Once/Week)	.46*** (.13)	.10 (.17)
Parental Education	.07 (.11)	-.21 (.15)
Parental Income	.01 (.05)	.02 (.07)
Social Media News User	.54† (.27)	-.29 (.38)
Political News Consumption	-.12 (.07)	.04 (.10)
White	.29 (.31)	.29 (.43)
Male	-.33 (.26)	.75* (.36)
R^2	.45	.27
n	87	87

OLS regression with robust standard errors in parentheses.

DV= Responses indicate agreement on a 7-point scale. 1= Strongly Disagree, 7=Strongly Agree

*** p<0.001, ** p<0.01, * p<0.05, † p<0.1

and fairly. In this instance, those respondents exposed to the race neutral folk treatment were more likely to agree that the police in this country treat everyone equally and fairly (p=.047). This finding seemingly contradicts expectations, given that the inclusion of this dependent variable is rooted in racial undertones associated with African Americans (i.e., racially coded language relating to the criminal justice system).

However, one must remember that rap is intrinsically linked to African Americans, and the evocation of rap music may activate racial considerations. If this is the case, respondents may experience dissonance with rap music failing to explicitly address race and/or experience the effect of social desirability bias. Specifically, respondents may feel compelled to respond in a "pro-Black" manner when race is primed implicitly via genre even if not lyrically addressed. Nevertheless, if this were the case, we would expect to see greater consistency across analyses involving rap manipulations.[38]

Racialized Americana-Folk versus Racialized Rap: The findings relating to the impact of the Americana-folk treatment versus rap when both address race and "One good way to teach certain people right from wrong is to give them a good stiff punishment when they get out of line" are presented in table 5.6. These results cast doubt on the notion that subtle racial priming via exposure to rap music results in more positive evaluations of African Americans. In this instance, those respondents receiving the Americana-folk treatment were significantly less likely to agree (p=.09) that a "good stiff punishment" is a way to teach "certain people" right from wrong than were those receiving the racialized rap treatment. This inverse finding suggests that racialized folk music can positively impact attitudes toward African Americans and potentially speaks to the dissonance associated with a stereotypically white medium compared to the stereotype-consistent Black medium in rap music.

The above findings also reveal a statistically significant inverse relationship with exposure to racialized Americana-folk versus racialized rap and level of agreement with negative evaluations of welfare recipients (p=.07). To this end, those receiving the racialized folk treatment were less likely to agree that welfare recipients prefer to live off welfare rather than being self-supporting compared to those receiving the rap treatment addressing race.

Americana-Rhythm and Blues: The impact of Americana music on political attitudes can be seen beyond the constituent folk genre. Specifically, exposure to the Americana-rhythm and blues treatment appears to have im-

Table 5.5. Americana-Folk Treatments vs. Rap (Race Neutral)

	Police can be Trusted to Treat Everyone Fairly and Equally
Treatment	.52* (.26)
Party Identification (6=Republican)	.50*** (.13)
Biblical Literalism (3=Literal Word of God)	.23 (.27)
Christian	.21 (.33)
Religious Attendance (5=>Once/Week)	-.09 (.12)
Parental Education	.06 (.11)
Parental Income	-.01 (.05)
Social Media News User	-.31 (.26)
Political News Consumption	-.05 (.07)
White	.17 (.36)
Male	.14 (.28)
R^2	.39
n	89

OLS regression with robust standard errors in parentheses.

DV= Responses indicate agreement on a 7-point scale. 1= Strongly Disagree, 7=Strongly Agree

*** p<0.001, ** p<0.01, * p<0.05, † p<0.1

Table 5.6. Americana-Folk Treatments vs. Rap (Racial Reference)

	Teach "Certain People" Right from Wrong with a "Good Stiff Punishment"	*Welfare Recipients Prefer to Live Off Welfare Rather than Being Self-Supporting*
Treatment	-.49† (.29)	-.57** (.31)
Party Identification (6=Republican)	-.14 (.13)	.18 (.14)
Biblical Literalism (3=Literal Word of God)	.24 (.31)	-.03 (.33)
Christian	-.13 (.37)	.46 (.39)
Religious Attendance (5=>Once/Week)	.24† (.14)	-.07 (.15)
Parental Education	-.18 (.13)	-.03 (.14)
Parental Income	.10† (.06)	-.01 (.06)
Social Media News User	.07 (.30)	-.22 (.31)
Political News Consumption	-.16† (.09)	.01 (.10)
White	.18 (.35)	.01 (.37)
Male	-.33 (.33)	.40 (.35)
R^2	.19	.14
n	85	85

OLS regression with robust standard errors in parentheses.

DV= Responses indicate agreement on a 7-point scale. 1= Strongly Disagree, 7=Strongly Agree

*** $p<0.001$, ** $p<0.01$, * $p<0.05$, † $p<0.1$

Table 5.7. Americana-Rhythm & Blues Treatments vs Commercial Country and Rap

Legal Immigrants Mostly Fill Jobs that U.S. Citizens Do Not Want

	Commercial Country (Racialized)	*Rap (Race Neutral)*	*Rap (Racialized)*
Treatment	.58* (.28)	.45† (.27)	.47† (.27)
Party Identification (6=Republican)	-.12 (.12)	-.16 (.12)	-.30** (.11)
Biblical Literalism (3=Literal Word of God)	.07 (.30)	.21 (.26)	-.11 (.29)
Christian	-.8* (.36)	-.73† (.38)	-.23 (.33)
Religious Attendance (5=>Once/Week)	.17 (.13)	.00 (.12)	.16 (.13)
Parental Education	.01 (.12)	.02 (.05)	.01 (.12)
Parental Income	-.01 (.05)	.28 (.30)	.01 (.05)
Social Media News User	.18 (.28)	.28 (.30)	.26 (.28)
Political News Consumption	-.05 (.08)	.04 (.07)	.00 (.09)
White	-.15 (.34)	-.02 (.38)	.06 (.32)
Male	-.09 (.32)	.28 (.30)	.51 (.32)
R^2	.16	.17	.19
n	101	91	98

OLS regression with robust standard errors in parentheses.

DV= Responses indicate agreement on a 7-point scale. 1= Strongly Disagree, 7=Strongly Agree

*** p<0.001, ** p<0.01, * p<0.05, † p<0.1

pacted attitudes toward immigrants when race is addressed as well as when race is not addressed. This impact can be seen in the race neutral rhythm and blues comparison to rap as well as the racialized comparisons to commercial country and rap. These results are illustrated in table 5.7.

In each of the three models presented in table 5.7, those respondents exposed to the Americana treatments were more likely to see legal immigrants as filling jobs that US citizens do not want than those respondents receiving manipulations featuring more popular music. The relationship is stronger, achieving statistical significance at the .05 level, when comparing the racialized Americana rhythm and blues and the commercial country treatments, however.

Caveats

While the results of the experimental analyses clearly reveal the ability of Americana music to impact attitudes toward minority groups, two caveats to the findings remain. First, attention must be paid to the unanticipated finding regarding exposure to the race neutral folk treatment as opposed to race neutral rap treatment relative to attitudes toward policing. Simply put, finding that respondents exposed to the race neutral folk treatment were more likely to agree that the police in this country treat everyone equally and fairly than were those receiving the race neutral rap treatment is perplexing, given theoretical expectations.

Second, despite an impressive seven of eight comparative analyses producing statistically significant results and only one failing to conform to expectations, the reader is cautioned that several models failed to produce statistically significant results regarding the experimental Americana treatments entirely.[39] Admittedly, finding the expected relationships across all analyses when so many are tested would be a high hurdle to clear. Nevertheless, the reader should be reminded that questions about impact remain.

Both of these caveats are addressed with greater detail in the final chapter of this book.

Opportunity for Impact

Despite the lingering questions noted above, testing the impact of exposure to Americana music on political attitudes via experimental design illustrates that this music has the ability to impact attitudes toward minorities. The experimental design has greater utility, however.

As noted above, respondents were asked about familiarity with the artist and the genre relative to the randomized treatment each received. They were similarly asked if they identified with and/or related to the music.[40] Given that popular forms of music tend to color the culture with which one identifies and that prior exposure to music may influence the ability of audiences to identify with or relate to the music and lyrics, I expect that those exposed to more widely disseminated music will more readily relate to that music when the music falls within racial expectations (i.e., white respondents receiving contemporary country music treatments and non-white respondents receiving rap treatments) than those receiving any of the Americana treatments. This was indeed the case, with greater than 60 percent of white respondents exposed to the race neutral commercial country treatment agreeing to varying levels of identification with or relation to the song. Greater than half (51.72 percent) of white respondents similarly reported identifying with or relating on some level with the racialized commercial treatment.

The non-white portion of the sample is nearly 76 percent African American. Expectantly, this subsample overwhelmingly identified with/related to both the rap treatments. Interestingly, this observation is more pronounced

Table 5.8. Identification with Commercial Country & Rap by Race

Treatment	*Non-White Agreement**	*White Agreement**
Race Neutral Commercial Country	25% (7)	60.87% (14)
Racialized Commercial Country	25% (5)	51.72% (15)
Race Neutral Rap	82.14% (23)	33.33% (7)
Racialized Rap	65.52% (19)	30.43% (7)

Note: Table reflects responses 4 (Somewhat Agree to Strongly Agree).

* Raw number of observations in parentheses.

for those non-white respondents receiving the race neutral treatment (82.14 percent) than those receiving the racialized treatment (65.52 percent).[41]

This research has established that Americana music may convey messaging inconsistent with stereotypes, and that Americana music is the foundation of a culture that may create at least partial dissonance with applicable stereotypes. Further, this chapter illustrates that the sample utilized in this research is largely unfamiliar with Americana. To that end, one could not expect the general "sound" of a music via instrumentation and/or intonation to instantly resonate with new listeners. Nevertheless, respondents exposed to one of the four Americana manipulations did indicate identification with/relation to the Americana treatments received. Table 5.9 illustrates these observations.[42]

While only a handful of white respondents indicate agreement with the statement "I identify/relate to the song" following exposure to the racialized folk treatment (importantly, only seventeen white respondents received this treatment), the table above clearly signals that both white and non-white respondents can identify with this music. Aside from white respondents receiving the race neutral rhythm and blues treatment and non-white respondents receiving the racialized rhythm and blues treatment, greater than 29 percent of respondents in six of the eight sample subgroups above signaled

Table 5.9. Identification with/Relation to Song

Americana Treatment	*Non-White Agreement**	*White Agreement**
Race Neutral Americana-Folk	50% (13)	36.35% (8)
Racialized Americana-Folk	32% (8)	29.41% (5)
Race Neutral Americana-Rhythm & Blues	33.33% (7)	15.52% (3)
Racialized Americana-Rhythm & Blues	15% (3)	69.70% (23)

Note: Table reflects responses 4 (Somewhat Agree to Strongly Agree).
* Raw number of observations in parentheses.

relating to the experimental manipulation they received. The racialized rhythm and blues treatment is notable, given the overwhelming agreement of white respondents and seemingly under-anticipated agreement among non-white respondents. However, the reader is cautioned that this finding likely results from consideration of the lyrics. While "White Man's World" clearly emphasizes the need for diversity by specifying white male privilege, the emphasis on lyrics that specify "white" repeatedly likely left non-white respondents that may have appreciated the sentiment identifying less with the song while white male respondents' sense of identity was clearly triggered. For instance, aside from the lyrics previously noted, this song includes "I'm a white man living on a white man's street" and "I'm a white man living in a white man's nation."[43]

This ability for unfamiliar audiences to relate to Americana music presents the opportunity for the messages of diversity conveyed through the music, the culture, or both to have a greater impact. Recognizing identification with the music signals the ability to stimulate in-group favoritism, which leads to more positive evaluations (see Tajfel and Turner 1979). In the case of this research, those more positive evaluations directly relate to messages of diversity and inclusion conveyed in this musical space.

Summary

This chapter details the eight treatments employed in the experimental analysis as well as the sample, which largely does not reflect the Americana community in demographic terms. Nevertheless, there is some overlap in leftist political attitudes between the sample and the Americana audience.

The analyses presented in this chapter reveal more positive evaluations of minority group members by those exposed to both racialized and race neutral Americana treatments compared to their relative counterparts in commercial country and rap music. However, the reader is reminded that this relationship failed to achieve statistical significance in the race neutral rhythm and blues comparison to race neutral commercial country. While there could be a number of explanations, similarities do exist between this variant of Americana and country music. Without context or socially progressive lyrics, respondents may have erroneously confused the music with country or even southern rock.

Nevertheless, underscoring the relationship between the Americana/roots music culture and diversity, the totality of the findings presented herein signal music associated with this culture as positively impacting attitudes toward African Americans, immigrants, and the LGBTQ+ community. Further, the descriptive statistics illustrating propensity for unfamiliar audiences to identify with and/or relate to Americana music emphasizes the ability of this music to serve as a tool to convey messages of diversity and inclusivity. This is notably the case relating to attitudes toward immigrants, where the impact can be seen across folk and rhythm and blues.

Despite hypotheses-confirming findings, the contrary result regarding attitudes toward police treatment deserves greater attention. Specifically finding that respondents exposed to the race neutral folk treatment were more likely to agree that the police in the United States treat everyone equally and fairly than were those receiving the race neutral rap treatment is antithetical to expectations. However, this finding may be related to the inclination of some to perceive folk music (at least in the United States) as intrinsically linked to protests and/or antiestablishment politics (e.g., Dunlap 2006). Certainly American folk music has long been connected to a sense of representing the downtrodden and oppressed (e.g., Dunaway and Beer 2010). Such an inherent connection rather than relevant racial considerations may then activate attitudes in some to express support for law enforcement.

Additional explanations may also potentially illuminate this perplexing finding regarding policing. For instance, while the young respondents utilized in this analysis are key to providing a study sample that contrasts with the Americana culture, young adults may respond to the prompt in an aspirational sense (i.e., they like to think that the police can be trusted to treat everyone equally and fairly). Similarly, they may not yet have the tools to see the connections between race and policing. Further, there is a propensity to view rap music as perpetually racialized. Finally, while the removal of the middle position eliminates the potential for participants to treat such a response as "Don't Know," it similarly encourages those participants who may be unaware of policing entirely to generate a response. This lack of awareness relating to policing may also explain the failure to produce statistically significant responses consistent with expectations across every experimental treatment featuring Americana music.

In turn, the reader should also recall that several models across these experimental conditions failed to produce statistically significant results regarding exposure to Americana music. This failure regarding welfare is particularly curious. There are only two statistically significant instances in which exposure to Americana music impacted attitudes toward welfare, and one of those is race neutral (i.e., race neutral Americana-folk). The other is the racialized rhythm and blues treatment. Given the convincing literature connecting attitudes toward welfare to negative racial attitudes (e.g., Gilens, 1996; 1999; Peffley, Hurwitz, and Sniderman 1997; Valentino 1999), failing to see significant results, particularly with regard to the racialized folk treatment, which specifically lyrically addresses poverty and African Americans, is particularly troublesome.

The following chapter turns to a collective consideration of artists' intent, the culture characterized by this music, and these experimental findings to provide a more holistic understanding of the relationship between Americana music and attitudes toward diversity.

›››››››› CONCLUSION ‹‹‹‹‹‹‹‹

THE LAST VERSE

In the light of introspection, where the truth is known to be.
It's our choices that betray us. It's the lie that says we're free.

—Reggie Harris, "It's Who We Are!" (2020)

This research has endeavored to unpack the potential political effects of Americana/roots music on attitudes relating to diversity and inclusion by considering the artists, the culture, and the impact of exposure to the music. Stereotype-incongruence and dissonance provide the theoretical framework that suggests that Americana/roots music has the ability to encourage more favorable attitudes toward minorities. Music, artists, and albums nominated for Americana Music Association awards between 2002 and 2021, the scope of the awards at the time of writing, represent the corpus of music thematically analyzed, while additional lyrics from artists in this space are offered for illustration so as not to bias presentation entirely toward nominated music.

Personal interviews with artists provide the core data for analyzing musical intent. These artist interviews as well as interviews with music writers, nonprofit executive directors/festival organizers, and a music director offer information relating to a secondary analysis of the community. Finally, I administered a survey-based experiment to college students in order to test the impact of Americana music exposure on unfamiliar listeners. Ultimately, the findings regarding artists, culture, and impact are summarized below:

1. Americana is best described as a culture or community in which roots music provides cohesion rather than purely as a musical genre;

2. While all artists do not embrace overtly political lyrics and/or address political sentiments during live performances, all see Americana as a space for socially aware lyrics and messaging to unfold;

3. Artists typically identify as moderate to progressive in terms of ideological predispositions, and they see their audiences as likely embracing similar political views. Many are clear, however, that they do not wish to contribute to partisan divides and welcome those with contrary opinions;

4. The Americana/roots music culture can generally be characterized as politically tolerant and empathic, but a visible minority of intolerant audience members is often evident;

5. The community is small and tight-knit in comparison to audiences of more commercial forms of music;

6. The community is older and predominately white; and

7. Exposure to Americana music tends to result in more positive attitudes toward minority group members.

These findings signal that roots music can be used as tools to impact attitudes rather than simply as a soundtrack to describe circumstances surrounding historical events. The remainder of these concluding remarks assesses that potential impact in light of three aspects of this research that deserve greater attention: the elitist nature of the culture, the role of women, and the overall potential impact of the music. After addressing each of these aspects, I consider an overarching concern about the ability of this music to have a broad impact beyond the community on attitudes toward minority groups. Specifically, if the insulated nature of the community allows for more thoughtful and contemplative social commentary, how can the music possibly maintain that impact to those outside the culture if reaching outsiders necessarily involves compromising on "small"?

* * *

Elitism

I was the chair and one of two discussants on a "Group Empathy" panel featuring research by several scholars, including Cigdem Sirin, Nicholas Valentino, and José Villalobos at the Midwest Political Science Association's annual meeting in 2019. An epigraph at the onset of the Sirin, Valentino, and Villalobos paper featured lyrics from Lucinda Williams's 2014 *Down Where the Spirit Meets the Bone* album.[1] Following the panel, I couldn't resist asking Dr. Valentino which scholar selected the lyrics. He gave credit to Dr. Sirin and added, "But, isn't she great?" in reference to Williams.

I subsequently contacted Dr. Sirin, who credited Dr. Villalobos, and further learned that both scholars are fans of Americana music, although they too enjoy trying to ascertain precisely what the music entails. Certainly, a collection of doctorate-holding political scientists seeking out this music speaks directly to Americana's appealing to the socially aware and/or highly educated. Similarly, my communication with Dr. Sirin reflects Colin Gilmore's belief that music builds community. Dr. Sirin is from Turkey, while I'm from southern Appalachia, and following our conversation about the impact of roots music she stated, "It's amazing how people with very different backgrounds can lead such parallel lives" (pers. interview, December 23, 2021). She is undoubtedly correct, and the music enabled us to relate to each other as much as our respective research.

This illustration of elitism should be applied cautiously, and the reader is again reminded that elite in this context should not be construed as "better than." Prior chapters have reinforced that the roots music audience is contemplative and socially aware, which should not necessarily be equated to advanced educational attainment. Some artists interviewed for this research as well as the music writers and the music director included herein characterize the majority of their fan bases and community members as college educated, but others are adamant that the community is exceedingly socially aware while levels of formal educational attainment are varied.

Nevertheless, the degree to which this culture embraces digging deeper into social, political, and historical narratives is worth highlighting. Moreover, investigating complicated and often uncomfortable subject matter relates to the culture's willingness to tackle the unclear and/or unpleasant. Americana's encouragement of deeper thinking of issues and greater introspection must not be confused with a willingness to contribute to partisan divides, however. As illustrated in previous chapters, artists interviewed for this research can be characterized as having varied approaches to partisan politics that range from largely apolitical to overtly partisan lyrical references that encourage listeners to vote (without specifying candidate and/or party preference), question, and become more informed about the issues occupying the midpoint on the hypothetical scale.

Darrell Scott's take on performance suggests that many Americana artists see virtue in ambivalence (pers. interview, April 21, 2021). He prefers to avoid set lists entirely. While familiar with this approach, he finds it leaves performing uncomfortable, which he sees as advantageous for the whole of the community. More specifically, the artist feels his/her/their way through performance while challenging the audience's expectations. Colin Gilmore similarly observes that one's ability to impact audiences is blunted if everyone consistently reacts to the performance and material in the same manner. He reasons that attendees can enjoy the show and have a good time if everyone is like-minded, but "Don't expect to have an impact" (pers. interview, December 21, 2021).

The roots music community could be seen as generally valuing impact over growth of audience. A narrowly focused small impact that allows the emphasis to remain on the music and the message is more important to artists in this culture than playing larger venues and cultivating a wider appeal. This interpretation, more often than not, results in artists in this space living as working musicians rather than enjoying the type of widespread commercial success Rodney Crowell experienced during his wildly lucrative career in popular country music. To that end, BettySoo reports that the artists in this culture willingly give up conventional measures of success, often including financial stability, for their art and the community (pers. interview, September 21, 2021). For his part, Crowell knowingly made this sacrifice, shifting his career away from commercial country music to Americana, where he feels he has an ongoing dialogue with his audience (pers. interview, March 3, 2021).

Women in Americana

The dramatically lower response rate from female artists as opposed to male artists contacted for this research as well as the combination of a dominance of straight white men and the older audience in Americana necessitates greater consideration of women in this space. Chapter 3 clearly articulates the difficulty in discerning why women may have been less inclined to participate in this research. However, observations of participating artists (both men and women) and others in this musical space, the descriptive results of the content analysis of Americana Music Association-nominated music, albums, and awards presented in chapter 1, and the discussion of the Americana culture addressed in chapter 4 provide relevant insights and point to fertile opportunities for future research.

To begin, all those interviewed are aware that women are underrepresented in Americana, and all are resultantly concerned. Some artists in this space, such as Jason Isbell, have the platform and resources to highlight women and minorities. Isbell played eight consecutive shows at the Ryman Auditorium in Nashville, Tennessee, in October 2021, with a woman as the opening act each night. Notably, seven of the eight women opening for Jason Isbell and the 400 Unit were women of color, including Shemekia Copeland, Mickey Guyton, Amythyst Kiah, Joy Oladokun, Allison Russell, Brittany Spencer, and Adia Victoria.[2] However, placing the onus of increasing the representation of women and/or racial ethnic minorities is often out of the hands of the artists themselves. Jason Isbell has achieved a level of critical success and recognition that eludes many male Americana artists, who are working musicians that must focus on their own professional and financial viability. Moreover, many of these men champion diversity and often write socially responsible lyrics. Therefore, the onus of increasing diversity in Americana cannot fall solely on the shoulders of straight white male artists.

Artists can convey messages of diversity and inclusion, but if venue owners, station managers, etc., do not make a similarly conscious effort, women and minorities will continue to be underrepresented.[3] Moreover, for audiences attracted to the stereotypical views of this music (i.e., hippies and cowboys), women may simply not fit into the molds, resulting in audiences being less inclined to consume their music or to seek out live performances by women.

Additionally, the age of the roots music audience and the propensity for the entertainment industry on the whole to promote a youth culture in live performances may limit the career time frame of those women that manage to find success in Americana. To this point, this audience is generally older, and they value authenticity. In turn, artists in their twenties, who are still finding their way musically and performatively and have fewer life experiences on which to draw from, are less likely to be embraced by this culture. Alternatively, when female artists reach their mid-fifties they are less likely to conform to a youth culture. This dynamic creates a high floor and a low ceiling for women that does not typically exist for their male counterparts.

Eliza Gilkyson, who was seventy-one when interviewed, explains this phenomenon by noting that some aspects of ageism creep into folk music even if the audience is older: "We are not held to the same standards as men. Older women are almost an embarrassment to a youth culture, whereas men become venerable. . . . You find yourself worrying about your aging face even as you evolve into your best work as an artist. It's frustrating. I have many times over the last twenty years had these 'come to Jesus' moments with myself where I just don't want to take the humiliation anymore, but I love making music too much and I can't imagine my life without it" (pers. interview, December 20, 2021). Gilkyson further states that she sees her place in the community as being available to "show younger women that we can be viable in our later years."

Bernice Lewis, sixty-eight at the time interviewed, similarly sees women as operating within tighter time constraints than men within this musical space (pers. interview, December 23, 2021).[4] Lewis expresses this notion of seeing one's perceived performance ability diminish with age lyrically in "Invisible" (2019): "I'm invisible. It's my superpower. It seems to grow much stronger every minute, every hour. Some folks leap tall buildings in a single bound and some of us just disappear without a sound."

Even younger women in Americana concur with Gilkyson. BettySoo says of Gilkyson's observation that women in this musical space work within a narrower time frame than male artists: "It's absolutely true" (pers. interview, December 29, 2021). Kristen Englenz, thirty-one when interviewed, adds that she sees more women becoming more visible as they age, however (pers. interview, December 29, 2021).

Notably, there may be niches within the broader community where ageism and sexism do not collide. Specifically, Jamie Anderson, who performs predominately for LGBTQ+ audiences and "a few brave straight guy fans" does not see age as having negatively impacted her career (pers. interview,

December 21, 2021). "I felt no rush to make an impact earlier, but then most of my fans are lesbians and age doesn't matter as much to them."

This research clearly points to a need to better investigate and understand women in Americana and roots music. In turn, future related studies should consider the impact of messages of diversity when delivered by female versus male artists as well as varying the age of artists. The latter is key in determining whether sex, age, and/or a combination of the two impacts the potency of messages in this musical space.

Musical Potency

Chapter 5 detailed the experimental design utilized to assess the impact of music associated with the Americana culture relative to attitudes toward minority groups. While participants were randomly exposed to eight treatments, four featured Americana music. These treatments include race neutral folk, racialized folk, race neutral rhythm and blues, and racialized rhythm and blues. Race neutral and racialized commercial country and rap treatments were also randomly administered and facilitated testing Americana's impact in relation to more popular forms of music. Chapter 5 also explicated the sample, which largely contrasts with the Americana culture in demographic terms.

Chapter 5 continued by providing the quantitative findings of the experimental analysis, which reveal that exposure to Americana music relates to increasingly positive assessments of minority groups. Specifically, these findings extend to African Americans, the LGBTQ+ community, and immigrants. Findings regarding the latter are particularly impressive, as they extend to increasingly positive assessments of legal immigrants by those exposed to folk and rhythm and blues treatments as well as race neutral and racialized treatments. Exposure to Americana music can generally be seen to have resulted in less support for racially coded measures of punishment and welfare, and those exposed to the racialized folk treatment were less likely to agree that gay marriage should not be legal.

Additionally, the descriptive findings concerning respondents' ability to identify with and/or relate to Americana music reported in chapter 5 provide further corroboration of the power of this music. Notable portions of both the white and non-white subsamples exposed to the folk and rhythm and blues treatments reported agreeing to some extent that they identify with and/or relate to the song. Increasing identification can then increase in-group favoritism, resulting in more positive evaluations of the music and associated targets.

While the experimental results clearly convey Americana music's ability to positively impact attitudes relating to diversity, and inclusion, there is greater utility in this research in the form of fruitful opportunities for additional research. Potential research questions that could lead to a better understanding of the Americana culture and the impact of associated music include but are not limited to the following:

1. Does the sex of the performing artist impact evaluations of minority groups and politics more generally?
2. Does the age of the performing artist impact evaluations of minority groups and politics more generally?
3. Does exposure to music within specific constituent genres have differing effects (e.g., gospel versus folk, bluegrass versus rhythm and blues)?
4. Are political/social attitudes other than those related to diversity and inclusion impacted by exposure to this music? and
5. Does the proliferation of audio sharing services, such as Pandora and Spotify, enable music associated with the Americana culture to reach a broader audience and potentially a greater impact?

The Rub

An exchange with Slaid Cleaves regarding the ambivalence Americana artists are often willing to take on in their writing led to the aforementioned "Rust Belt Fields." I often find myself returning to this song after Rod Picott addressed differing interpretations. The salute to the common man I hear in the song from Cleaves's 2013 *Still Fighting the War* album and Picott's 2011 *Welding Burns* album is not laced with attitudes toward immigration and free market enterprise, but that's shortsighted of me. Cleaves understands the draw to the song despite differing interpretations: "As grandiose as it sounds, I suspect if songs like these, that tell the stories of struggling people and struggling towns, were on the radio as much as 'Bro Country' or whatever else was on the radio, then some people would've felt less forgotten and perhaps wouldn't have voted so nihilistically in 2016" (pers. interview, December 29, 2021). Indeed, the lyrics "No one gets a bonus for bloody knuckles and scars. No one remembers your name just for working hard" transcend partisan divides.

Furthermore, I can't prevent myself from personalizing the song by relating it to coal mining despite lyrics referencing factory work. I was raised in a community rooted in the coal industry. I learned to drive on narrow, serpentine roads, often without guardrails, that weaved through mountains with flat tops and unnatural, perfectly stacked ridges that signaled strip mining had occurred. Coal tipples were a permanent landscape aesthetic to appreciate during one's commute, when trains transporting countless coal cars would frequently pause, reverse, and move forward simply to repeat the process minutes later. Hard rains initially brought black dust, and subsequently dark water would fill ditches and eventually seep beneath the ground. Coal colored the community to the point it literally colored the water, and then the laundry.

Despite the frequent travel delays and need for bottled water, I understood as a child that coal was integral to life. Mining brought new people and ancillary businesses in the form of companies designed to provide the equipment necessary for mining, and additional businesses designed to support the influx of new residents. I also became aware that when the mining industry dwindled, businesses closed, jobs were lost, and people left. As I aged and came to understand the dangers of ostensibly centering an entire community on a nonrenewable resource, I continually fought dissonance with coal.

As an adult I retain a lot of associated ambivalence related to coal mining. I see the needs for job training in completely separate industries and greater social capital (see Couto 1999; Putnam 2000). I understand environmental dangers, and have seen the craters, pits, snaking treacherous paths, and, yes, "falling rock" warning signs that adorn what were once, in an era long before my birth, majestic mountains covered by a green canopy created from a mix of pine and oak trees.

When I hear Slaid Cleaves or Rod Picott sing "Rust Belt Fields," I *hear* "factory," but I *see* the soot-covered coal miner coming home from work.

I think about the juxtaposition of my children's present need for outdoor showers so they don't track sand through the house after a day at the beach and the need for coal miners to have outdoor or basement showers with a separate home entrance so coal soot doesn't lurk into carpet and upholstery. Cleaves and Picott drudge the conflicting emotions such that I understand the connection between factory workers, coal miners, auto workers, etc. So Slaid, your interpretation of the song is not as much grandiose as it is apt.

Nevertheless, Cleaves's comment about playing similar music on the radio illustrates the greater rub with Americana culture. The small, insular community provides artists with the room necessary to experiment, grow, and challenge listeners. If this music were more widely disseminated, one has to ask whether it would retain potency. Darrell Scott's work suggests this is the case, given that several of his songs have been covered by prominent commercial country musicians, such as Faith Hill, Alan Jackson, Patty Loveless, Brad Paisley, and Travis Tritt. Even Beyonce sampled the Dixie Chicks covering Scott's "Long Time Gone" (2000) on her *Lemonade* (2016) album. Despite Scott's example, however, Americana artists across constituent genres do not tend to see their work covered by more commercially successful acts.

In turn, one has to wonder what the impact would be if this music were easier to locate. Scott's understanding that keeping Americana small allows the product to remain pure is well-founded. When commercially successful artists such as Rodney Crowell and even Led Zepplin's Robert Plant venture into Americana, they adapt. Additionally, the Americana community has grown by most objective measures since the time of *Honky Tonk Amnesia,* the inception of the Americana charts, and the establishment of the Americana Music Association while managing to keep costs relatively low and continuing to support artists in smaller venues and even house concerts.

Concluding Thoughts

The epigraph at the onset of this conclusion reflects Reggie Harris's 2020 "It's Who We Are!" Additional lyrics from the song include, "It's a universal struggle. One fed by vicious lies. We've all been bought and sold for someone else's gain. It's a mystical dilemma. It's a puzzle that defies our attempts to put the pieces in the frame." Harris speaks to politics, media, and human nature in the song (and indeed his life's work). In some ways, the task of this research mirrors the goal of Harris's work. This study has considered the intersection of cognitive processes and exposure to Americana music and the resultant impact on political attitudes, specifically as those attitudes relate to diversity and inclusion. Therefore, this study presents the puzzle pieces, yet work remains before the framing.

I am ultimately left asking how one goes about using this tool to promote messages of diversity, inclusion, and beyond. This research clearly illustrates the ability of music within the Americana culture to impact unfamiliar audiences and stimulate more positive evaluations of minority group members. However, determining how to disseminate the music widely without compromising artists' intent in order to have a more sizeable impact is beyond the scope of this research.

NOTES

Foreword

1. This statement can be found at www.obamawhitehouse.archives.gov.

2. See www.guydavis.com for more information.

Introduction: The Downhome Sound

1. Todd Snider, *Songs for the Daily Planet* (1994).

2. Robbie Robertson, "Up on Cripple Creek" (1969).

3. Joel Rafael likewise describes his experiences with the 1960s counterculture movement as somewhere that everyone was welcome. This is further addressed in chapter 4.

4. Finnan's tenure with FAI concluded in 2022.

5. Bob Dylan, "Blowin' in the Wind" (1962).

6. Chester Burnett, "How Many More Years?" (1951).

7. John Prine, "Sabu Visits the Twin Cities Alone" (1978).

8. Pete Seeger and Lee Hayes, "If I Had a Hammer" (1950).

9. Jason Isbell, "White Man's World" (2017).

10. This was a weekly radio program known as *Honky Tonk Amnesia* broadcasted from KCSN, the public radio station associated with California State University, Northridge.

11. For more information related to the origin of the Americana Music Association, see https://americanamusic.org/node/495.

12. Slaid Cleaves and Rod Picott, "Welding Burns" (2013).

13. John and Alan Lomax's *American Ballads and Folk Songs* and *Our Singing Country: Folk Songs and Ballads* very clearly illustrates the influence of the Negro spiritual on American folk music.

14. https://folk.org/about/.

15. Alan Lomax, *Negro Prison Songs from the Mississippi State Penitentiary* (1947).

16. Waylon Jennings, Willie Nelson, Jessie Colter, and Tompall Glasser, *Wanted! The Outlaws* (1976).

17. Phil Barker, "Underdog" (2018).

18. Cody Jinks, "Hippies and Cowboys" (2017).

1. The First Verse

1. Keb' Mo' collaborated with Roseanne Cash on "Put a Woman in Charge" on *Oklahoma* in 2019. Keb' Mo' released "The Medicine Man" with Old Crow Medicine Show in 2021.

2. Further consideration of racially coded language is included in chapter 5 in relation to dependent variable selection.

3. Each of these theories varies based on motivation (e.g., preservation of existing racial order as addressed by Bonilla-Silva [see also Bonilla-Silva and Dietrich 2011]), but all couch anti-Black attitudes in terms of morality, ideals, and culture rather than biological inferiority.

4. *Racism without Racists: Color-Blind Racism and the Persistence of Racial Inequality in America* is currently in its fifth edition. The first edition is cited here.

5. Fitzgerald and Green (2017) provide a summary discussion of narrative transportation theory.

6. Rap music is used in comparison because it is stereotype-confirming, but it is not addressed at length here given that the focus is on the stereotype-disconfirming genre. Nevertheless, rap music is more thoroughly addressed in chapters 4 and 5.

7. Each nomination is treated as a separate observation. Individual acts/artists may, therefore, constitute multiple observations within and across years. Also, Emerging Act of the Year was not a separate award category in the first two years of the Americana Music Awards. Similarly, Duo/Group of the Year and Lifetime Achievement for Instrumentalist were added as separate categories in 2006. There was no Lifetime Achievement Award for Instrumentalist in 2016, 2019, or 2020 and no Lifetime Achievement Award for Songwriting in 2018 and 2020, and no Lifetime Achievement Award for Performance in 2020, however.

8. Artists performing as part of a group/duo and individually are treated as separate observations unless only one artist is named with a band. For instance, Buddy Miller was nominated once for song of the year as a solo artist and once with his wife, Julie Miller. Alternatively, when individual artists are clearly given standing apart from other group members, they are treated collectively. For example, Jason Isbell is treated as having five total nominations for his work solo and his work fronting Jason Isbell and the 400 Unit. Similarly, Nathaniel Rateliff has two nominations, one as a solo act and one fronting Nathaniel Rateliff and the Night Sweats.

9. *Caught in the Webb: A Tribute to the Legendary Webb Pierce* was nominated for album of the year in 2002 and *This One's for Him: A Tribute to Guy Clark* was nominated in 2012. Both albums won, but both featured multiple artists and the latter consisted of three volumes.

10. This figure is achieved by considering separate performers. Therefore, instances where artists perform in different groups, duos, etc. are treated as separate observations. For example, Buddy Miller was nominated singularly twelve times; he was also nominated three times with Julie Miller, once with Jim Lauderdale, and once with Robert Plant and the Band of Joy. Therefore, his nominations represent seventeen observations.

11. Where public statements relating to homosexual orientation are absent, heterosexuality is assumed.

12. Brandi Carlile, Brittany Howard, Mary Gauthier, and Amythyst Kiah were each nominated for Song of the Year. The fifth observation is by The Highwomen, which features three heterosexual women (Natalie Hemby, Maren Morris, and Amanda Shires) in addition to Carlile.

13. See Freeman (2021) for an interview in which Tasjan addresses his sexual orientation.

14. Duos/groups are coded as racial/ethnic minorities if one or more group member can be characterized as such.

15. Cooper (2020) addresses Crockett's heritage through an interview with *The Guardian,* and notes that Crockett's roots are Black, Cajun, Creole, and Jewish.

16. Keb' Mo' received the Lifetime Achievement Award for Performance. The Mavericks, a band with Latinx roots, was recognized with the Americana Trailblazer Award. African American Carla Thomas received the Americana Inspiration Award.

2. The Music

1. Maya Angelou, "I Know Why the Caged Bird Sings" (1969).

2. Julie Miller is the author of "Midnight and Lonesome," but the song is performed by and appears on her husband, Buddy Miller's 2002 album of the same name.

3. Concurring Opinion in *Jacobellis v. Ohio,* 378 U.S. 184 (1964).

4. I became familiar with this term while interviewing Tim O'Brien on February 24, 2021. The phrase is used with some frequency, but the origin is unknown.

5. Refer to the US Department of Agriculture's 2020 agriculture and food statistics. USDA Economic Research Service, Ag and Food Statistics: Charting the Essentials, https://www.ers.usda.gov/data-products/ag-and-food-statistics-charting-the-essentials/.

6. Evan Felker, "Before the Devil Knows We're Dead" (2012).

7. Despite Tichi's (1994) description of country music as "American music," I do not include album or song titles that specifically state "America(n)" or any national derivative. While Americana music addresses regions with specificity, "the heartland" necessitates dividing the country for analytic purposes. Additionally, nationalism (conceived as exclusionary) can be seen as antithetical to contemporary Americana music.

8. Lori McKenna, Natalie Hemby, and Brandi Carlile, "Crowded Table" (2019).

9. Gillian Welch, "I Want to Sing that Rock and Roll" (2001).

10. Patterson Hood, "Thoughts and Prayers" (2020).

11. Hayes Carll and Brian Keene, "She Left Me for Jesus" (2008).

12. Hank Williams and Fred Rose, "I'll Never Get Out of this World Alive" (1954).

13. Chester Burnett, "How Many More Years" (1954).

14. Todd Snider, "Beer Run" (2005).

15. Jesse Langlais, "Life and Debt" (2018).

16. See John Dominis's 1964 twelve-page pictorial in *Life* magazine, "The Valley of Poverty."

17. Consult Food and Research Action Center 2017 data. See the FRAC's "Poverty Rates by Congressional District" map, https://frac.org/maps/acs-poverty/acs-poverty.html.

18. Jason Isbell, "Alabama Pines" (2012), Michael Trent Robinson and Cary Ann Hearst, "Birmingham" (2013), and Jason Isbell, "Cover Me Up" (2014), all won the Song of the Year category. Tyler Childers's "A Long Violent History" was nominated in 2021.

19. Michael Trent Robinson and Cary Ann Hearst, "Birmingham" (2013).

20. Milt Okun, Peter Yarrow, Noel Paul Stookey, Mary Travers, "Tell It on the Mountain" (1963).

21. Scott David, John Evans, and Hayes Carll, "KMAG YOYO" (2011); Elizabeth Cook and Melinda Schneider, "It Takes Balls to Be a Woman" (2007); Steve Earle, "The Revolution Starts . . . Now" (2005).

22. The "By Degrees" nominated recording features songwriter Mark Erelli, Lori McKenna, Roseanne Cash, Sheryl Crow, Anais Mitchell, and Josh Ritter. Ondara sang the verse sang by Crow on the recording during the awards ceremony.

23. See, for instance, Todd Snider's song "Thin Wild Mercury" from his 2006 album *The Devil You Know,* which includes the lyrics "It was all over some new Dylan song that Phil had the nerve to say sounded wrong. Dylan stopped the car, words shook like a fist. 'Phil you ain't a writer, you're a journalist.'"

24. Phil Ochs, "How High's the Watergate?" (1974).

25. James McMurtry, "Cheney's Toy" (2008).

26. Slaid Cleaves Livestream January 2021 Edition, YouTube, https://www.youtube.com/watch?v=XwpjSHJlUTs.

27. Slaid Cleaves, "Justice" (1990).

28. A discussion of the circumstances surrounding the Liberty conviction can be found at "'Donald Trump with a Maine Accent' Sentenced to Four Months for Illegal Campaign Donations," https://bangordailynews.com/2017/08/09/news/donald-trump-with-a-maine-accent-sentenced-to-four-months-for-illegal-campaign-donations/.

29. Michael Trent Robinson and Cary Ann Hearst, "C'Mon, Utah" (2019).

30. See description available at Shovels and Rope-All Eyes Media, https://alleyesmedia.com/clients/shovels-and-rope/.

31. Slaid Cleaves and Rod Picott, "Rust Belt Fields" (2011).

32. Jim Lauderdale, "She's Looking at Me" (200); Robert Ellis, "The Light from the Chemical Plant" (2014).

33. Mick Jagger and Keith Richards, "Dead Flowers" (1970).

34. John Prine, "The Late John Garfield Blues" (1972).

35. Todd Snider, *Time as We Know It: The Songs of Jerry Jeff Walker* (2012). Contributors to *This One's for Him: A Tribute to Guy Clark* (2011) include Terry Allen, Suzy Boggus, Shawn Camp, Hayes Carll, Roseanne Cash, Shawn Colvin, Rodney Crowell, Steve Earle, Ramblin' Jack Elliott, Joe Ely, Rosie Flores, Radney Foster, Vince Gill, Patty Griffin, Emmylou Harris, Terri Hendrix, Ray Wylie Hubbard, Jack Ingram, Robert Earl Keen, Kris Kristofferson, Lyle Lovett, James McMurtry, Willie Nelson, Gary Nicholson, Tim O'Brien, John Prine, Darrell Scott, The Trishas, Verlon Thompson, Townes Van Zandt, Jerry Jeff Walker, and Kevin Welch.

36. "Betty Was Black (and Willie Was White)" appeared on Todd Snider's *Happy to Be Here* (2000). The song also appeared on the Bis-Quits 1993 self-titled album.

37. Canada continues to sing "Betty Was Black" with The Departed and as a solo act.

3. The Artists

1. Rodney Crowell, "It Ain't Over Yet" (2017).

2. See Saviano's *Without Getting Killed or Caught* for a detailed biography of Guy Clark.

3. Artists, journalists, executive directors, and other individuals interviewed for this book were not compensated financially for their participation.

4. While artists of color were contacted, they or their representatives either failed to respond and/or the artist was unavailable. Initial contact was made via email to management and/or publicists. Given that these associations change, it is possible that many email solicitations were not received.

5. Multiple artists interviewed have musicians in their families. Notably, Colin Gilmore's father, Jimmie Dale Gilmore, is a member of the Flatlanders. The Flatlanders' "Homeland Refugee" was nominated for Song of the Year by the Americana Music Association in 2009.

6. See "President Trump Visits St. John's Church, Holds Up Bible" at *RealClear Politics* for discussion of Trump's appearance at St. John's Episcopal Church.

7. David Olney, Anana Katsadaze, and Irakli Gaprindashvili, "The Last Days of Rome" (2018).

8. Tim O'Brien was first nominated for a Grammy in 1990 for Best Bluegrass Recording. He was also nominated for Best Bluegrass Album in 1996, Best Country Instrumental Performance in 2000, Best Traditional Folk Album in 2005, Best American Roots Song in 2013, and Best Bluegrass Album in 2014. He won in 2005 for Best Traditional Folk Album with *Fiddler's Green* and again in 2014 for Best Bluegrass Album with *The Earls of Leicester*.

9. *The Gavin Report*, 1992, "Gavin Celebrates American Music: The Singer/Songwriter Issue," no. 1912.

10. Garland Jeffries and Jules Shear were also listed.

11. For a concise time line of the foundation of the Highlander Folk School (now the Highlander Research and Education Center), visit https://highlandercenter.org/our-history-timeline/.

12. Greater information about Songwriting with Soldiers can be found at https://www.songwritingwithsoldiers.org/.

13. Rafael's father was successful in securing the school board position, and he reports the bus walk-off was a failure that was likely upended by the newspaper alerting the school principal. He was suspended from school as a result.

14. Bob Dylan, "The Death of Emmett Till" (1962).

15. More information about the Underground Railroad program can be found at https://reggieharrismusic.com/education/ and http://www.kimandreggie.com/ugrr.htm.

16. Gary Stewart recorded "I Ain't Living Long Like This" in 1977. Lee Ann Womack released "Ashes by Now" in 2003, Wynonna Judd recorded "Sing" in 2009, and Patty Loveless released her version of "Lovin' All Night" in 2003. Crowell and Harris have collaborated for decades, including her 1978 release of Crowell and Donivan Cowart's "Leaving Louisiana in the Broad Daylight" (which was also recorded by the Oak Ridge Boys and later Americana duo Shovels and Rope) and "Even Cowgirls Get the Blues" the same year.

17. See Billboard's Hot 100 Chart, https://www.billboard.com/charts/hot-100/.

18. Crowell wrote, produced, and performed on *Lifted Off the Ground*. Will Kimbrough also performed on the album.

19. In six cases, artist contact information was provided by other artists. In each of those instances, the second artist agreed to the interview. In three additional cases, contact information was provided through association with the Kerrville Folk Festival executive director (Mary Muse). Each of these three artists agreed to an interview. Thus, none of twenty-three artists was reached via a secondary contact.

20. Diversity of audience was addressed in each interview. Diversity across artists was not. This grew organically throughout the interview process when I addressed lack of response by female artists and/or their representatives. In turn, generalizations about the group may apply to subsets of the sample.

21. WDVX is a nonprofit, listener-supported station specializing in roots music broadly and Bluegrass and folk music specifically. It broadcasts from Knoxville, Tennessee. In addition to serving as music director, Gullet hosts two programs on WDVX: *Americana Pulse* and *This Week in Americana.* More information about WDVX can be found at https://wdvx.com/about/.

4. The Community

1. A discussion can be found at www.youtube.com/watch?v=SljGCDNoEuQ.

2. Tim O'Brien, "He Walked On," 2021. Bloody Sunday refers to a series of events following the preventable death of youth civil rights leader Jimmie Lee Jackson. Peaceful protestors, led by John Lewis among others, marched across Edmund Petus Bridge on March 7, 1965, but met resistance from Alabama State Troopers and others who utilized horsemen and tear gas and assaulted protestors, which resulted in injury. The event drew support for the 1965 Voting Rights Act. For greater detail, see https://www.nps.gov/semo/learn/historyculture/bloody-sunday.htm.

3. House concerts are performances held in individual homes at the expense of the homeowner and/or volunteers. While these performances could contribute to cultural insularity and are largely advertised via social media and/or word of mouth, they represent only one venue in this musical space.

4. City Winery is a venue chain with eight locations in the United States as of August 2022.

5. See "James McMurtry's Continental Riffs," *No Depression,* https://www.nodepression.com/james-mcmurtrys-continental-riffs/.

6. See Hubbard's interview in Durcholz (2018); Jerry Jeff Walker, *Viva Terlingua!* (1973)

7. Stouffer considered respondents' support for "a communist making a speech in your community."

8. "Sam Stones" refers to John Prine's 1971 song "Sam Stone" on his self-titled album.

9. This single item on a fourteen-item index is used to illustrate the relationship between group empathy and this research. Addressing the full domain of the index is beyond the scope of this research.

10. See "Tim O'Brien and Jan Fabricius 'Sodbuster' WDVX Live From Home" (2021), *YouTube,* May 6, 2021, for the performance; Bill Caswell, "Sod Buster" (1980).

11. Personal communication (December 19, 2021) with one of the "Frank Empathy" artists, Doug Brumley, revealed that a majority of individuals contacting the artists about this artwork can be characterized professionally as either musicians, librarians, or booksellers.

12. Gilkyson specifically points to the success that artists such as Jason Isbell and Brandi Carlile have in bringing roots music to the American South.

13. BettySoo (winner and later judge), Slaid Cleaves (winner and later judge), Aengus Finnan (winner and later judge), Eliza Gilkyson (judge), Bernice Lewis (finalist and later judge), Joel Rafael (finalist and later winner). For New Folk winners, finalists, and judges,

see "Kerrville Folk Festival New Folk Finalist History," https://www.kerrvillefolkfestival.org/history-of-newfolk.

14. Kimbrough notes, in an interview with *The Bluegrass Situation,* that his friend who he references in the song referred to him as his "Left Wing Friend." See BGS Staff (2020), "LISTEN: Will Kimbrough, 'My Right Wing Friend,'" *The Bluegrass Situation,* September 10, 2020.

15. Buford Pusser was a Tennessee sheriff known for persecution of organized crime. He survived multiple assassination attempts (including one that left his wife dead) and was the inspiration for the 1973 film *Walking Tall.* See W. R. Morris's *Buford: The True Story of "Walking Tall" Sheriff Buford Pusser* (1983) for more details. Ramon Casiano was a Hispanic teenager murdered by then-teenaged Harlan Carter in 1931. Casiano was armed with a knife, while Carter was armed with a gun (see Smith 2017). Carter would go on to work for the US Border Patrol and became infamous for shifting the direction of the NRA from marksmanship and safety to uncompromising gun rights.

16. Eliza Gilkyson made the point of noting that a sustainable living can be made in folk music during the personal interview conducted on April 8, 2021.

17. Michael Trent Robinson and Cary Ann Hearst, "St. Anne's Parade" (2016).

5. The Impact

1. Qualtrics is an experience management company that caters to a variety of businesses and nonprofits by offering platforms for survey-based research and cloud-based storage.

2. The survey was also administered at Augusta University and Purdue University Northwest.

3. Valdosta State University is located in southern Georgia, and Lewis University is located in Illinois. Despite the inclusion of a midwestern university and Tennessee Technological University, a sizeable majority of respondents (276) identified Georgia as their home state. Florida was unsurprisingly the second most identified home state (44), as Valdosta State University is less than eighteen miles from Florida.

4. The first and second waves were administered in a relatively brief period of time. In turn, given the number of experimental treatments and smaller sample size in the second wave, this analysis does not control for wave in the analyses below. Doing so would result in very few second observations across treatments.

5. VSU institutional enrollment statistics for spring 2021 can be found at https://www.valdosta.edu/administration/institutional-research/documents/enrollment-graduation-retention/enrollment_spring_2021.pdf. VSU institutional enrollment statistics for summer 2021 can be found at https://www.valdosta.edu/administration/institutional-research/documents/enrollment-graduation-retention/enrollment_summer_2021.pdf.

6. While individual professors at participating institutions may have offered additional points on graded work for survey completion, this decision was left to those professors. Participants were provided with a completion code via Qualtrics upon completion to confirm participation while ensuring confidentiality. Participants were not monetarily compensated.

7. The dramatic juxtaposition between male and female response rates (women comprise nearly 70 percent of the sample) is not reflective of the respective university populations. One

might anticipate that males are less inclined to complete surveys; however, the data collected for this research do not allow for the testing of that assumption.

The survey specifically asked "biological sex" rather than "gender" or "gender identity." The decision to include this question as well as a question that addressed transgendered identity was made in order to parse out differences in the transgender population, given concerns about participant knowledge of the term "cisgender" (i.e., do transmen posit differing attitudes/behaviors than transwomen and/or biological males; do transwomen posit differing attitudes/behaviors than transmen and/or biological women). However, only two respondents identified as transgender. One reported being biologically male; one reported identifying as biologically female.

8. The survey instrument specified "Protestant Christian (Baptist, Episcopalian, Methodist, Presbyterian, etc.)." Respondents were not asked to provide specific denominational affiliation.

9. Those identifying as Christian (both Protestants and Catholics) report attending religious services more often than those affiliating with other religions. Specifically, nearly 59 percent of Christians sampled report attending religious services monthly or more compared to less than 14 percent of non-Christians. One should note, however, that options for religious services maybe limited for those respondents not identifying as Christian. For example, Valdosta, Georgia, is home to countless Christian churches. Indeed, students at Valdosta State University could easily walk to a number of Christian churches from campus (including an Episcopal church that faces campus and provides student housing); however, there are no Buddhist or Hindu temples in the city. Unsurprisingly, those identifying as not ascribing to a particular religion report less frequent religious attendance.

10. See also Kellstedt (1989) for a more general discussion of the impact of evangelicalism and biblical literalism.

11. See Sears (1986) for a discussion of limitations associated with the use of student samples.

12. Given the difficulty in ranking education degrees post bachelor's degree (e.g., Should all terminal degrees be assessed similarly?), care is taken to address advanced degrees collectively insofar as possible.

13. Respondent best estimate of parental/guardian income was also collected. However, it is not presented in text. This information is presented in graph 5.1. The modal category on the ordinal scale offered is "Greater than $100,000," which was reported by more than 18 percent of respondents. Parental income is utilized as a control variable in the analyses presented in the following chapter.

14. Respondents were instructed at the onset of the survey that skipping questions was permitted.

15. While youth voting is generally low, age is a factor in eligibility for voting for this sample, as is the persistent factor of college students' lack of information regarding precinct location and vote-by-mail options.

16. In addition to asking about the 2020 presidential election, respondents were also asked about the 2021 run-off election in Georgia, given the inclusion of Valdosta State University students in the sample. Approximately 32 percent of respondents indicated "Did Not Vote/Ineligible to Vote" for this question.

17. Participants were not able to advance to the post-stimulus questions until time sufficient for the song to conclude elapsed.

18. Qualtrics randomly varied treatments while ensuring that treatments were presented to participants in approximately equal proportions.

19. While lyrical content and limited prior exposure to the artist may signal country music to listeners unfamiliar with the Americana label, rhythm and blues and rock are unmistakable in the selections. Indeed, Sullivan (2013) characterizes "Super 8" as a "full-throttle raver" and Gage (2018) refers to "White Man's World" as "blazing."

20. Jeffrey Steele and Davis Naish, "Stick That in Your Country Song" (2015).

21. Detroit, Michigan, is greater than 78 percent African American. See https://www.census.gov/quickfacts/detroitcitymichigan.

22. Eric Church, Jeff Hyde, and Ryan Tyndall, "Springsteen" (2012).

23. See Barack Obama and Bruce Springsteen, *Renegades* (2021).

24. Jermaine Cole and Anthony Parrino, "Folgers Crystals" (2015).

25. *Rolling Stone* further ranked *Southeastern* #458 on their list of the top 500 albums of all time. See https://www.rollingstone.com/music/music-lists/best-albums-of-all-time-1062063/.

26. While some political attitudes were collected prior to exposure to the treatment, those measures are not utilized in this research as dependent variables.

27. "Things Have Changed" appears on multiple Dylan albums in addition to the 2000 *Wonder Boys* soundtrack. These albums include *The Essential Bob Dylan* (2000), *The Best of Bob Dylan* (2005), *Dylan* (2007), and *The Bootleg Series,* vol. 8, *Tell Tale Signs* (2008).

28. Bob Dylan's Academy Awards acceptance speech can be found at http://aaspeechesdb.oscars.org/link/073-15/.

29. Bob Dylan and Jacques Levy, "The Hurricane" (1975). "The Hurricane" refers to Rubin Carter, a Black man wrongfully convicted of murder. For a synopsis and link to Dylan, see "Rubin 'Hurricane' Carter, Boxer Who Inspired Bob Dylan, Dies at 76," https://www.billboard.com/music/music-news/rubin-hurricane-carter-boxer-who-inspired-bob-dylan-dies-at-76-6062703/.

30. Nathaniel Rateliff, "It's Still Alright" (2020).

31. None of the measures utilized here ask about minority group attitudes directly, given concerns about social desirability bias as explained in the text. Policy and related attitudes concerning immigrants and the LGBTQ+ community are addressed directly. More subtle language is used to address African Americans. This decision was made given extant research supporting symbolic racism (e.g., Henry and Sears 2002; Kinder and Sears 1981; Sears 1988), subtle racism (e.g., Pettigrew and Meertens 1995), and modern racism (e.g., McConahay 1986), all of which suggest that white Americans express true attitudes toward African Americans' policy preferences through policy attitudes. More specifically, each of these concepts implies that whites see Blacks as violating American values.

32. While sexual orientation could theoretically impact each of the dependent variables, particularly attitudes toward gay marriage, this control is not utilized. The sample nonheterosexual population is relatively large (20 percent), and the random dispersion of nonheterosexual identifying respondents across experimental manipulation leaves five of eight experimental treatments with ten or fewer LGBTQ+ respondents.

33. The recoding of parental education is 1 = High School Degree or Less, 2 = Associate De-

gree and/or Technical College, 3 = Some College at a 4-year college or university, 4 = Bachelor's Degree, 5 = >Bachelor Degree. While this approach may fail to capture some of the nuance of certain graduate degrees versus terminal degrees requiring greater training, such as the M.D. and Ph.D., it avoids the complications of assigning "greater than" to graduate degrees in diverse disciplines that may not have educational equivalents.

34. This result reflects 27.5 percent of models tested.

35. As noted in the previous chapter, those exposed may detect country music undertones.

36. .1 is used as a low threshold for each of the two-tailed tests presented in this chapter.

37. This model produces an impressively high (in relative terms for survey analyses) R^2 goodness of fit statistic, >.45, implying that greater than 45 percent of variance is explained by the linear model.

38. Greater speculation about this intriguing relationship can be found in the summary of this chapter and in the concluding chapter of this research.

39. Again, exposure to race-neutral Americana-rhythm and blues compared to race-neutral commercial country was not significantly related to any of the five dependent variables specified in this analysis.

40. The prompt for this question is, "I identify/relate to this song." Responses ranged from Strongly Disagree (1) to Strongly Agree (6).

41. See table 5.8.

42. Identification with/relation to the music in the experimental treatment is not used as a control in the regression analyses, as its inclusion diminished subsample size across treatments.

43. Jason Isbell, "White Man's World" (2017).

Conclusion: The Last Verse

1. The same epigraph is now featured in their 2021 book, *Seeing Us in Them: Social Divisions and the Politics of Group Empathy.*

2. Isbell's wife, Amanda Shires, was the first opening act of this set of eight shows.

3. Refer to Aengus Finnan's related discussion in chapter 4.

4. Personal interview conducted December 23, 2021.

REFERENCES

Allcott, Hunt, and Matthew Gentzkow. 2017. "Social Media and Fake News in the 2016 Presidential Election." *Journal of Economic Perspectives* 31: 211–236.

Allport, Gordon. 1954. *The Nature of Prejudice.* Reading, Mass.: Addison-Wesley.

Althaus, Scott L. 1998. "Information Effects in Collective Preferences." *American Political Science Review* 99: 153–167.

Americana Music Association. 2021. "The History of the Americana Music Association." https://americanamusic.org/node/495.

Anderson, Jamie. 2019. *An Army of Lovers: Women's Music of the Seventies and Eighties.* Tallahassee, Fla.: Bella Books.

Auxier, Brooke, and Monica Anderson. 2021. "Social Media Use in 2021." *Pew Research Center.* April 7, 2021. Social Media Use in 2021, Pew Research Center

Barth, Jay, L. Marvin Overby, and Scott H. Huffmon. 2009. "Community Context, Personal Contact, and Support for an Anti-Gay Rights Referendum." *Political Research Quarterly* 62: 355–365.

Becker, Ernest. 1971. *The Birth and Death of Meaning.* New York: Free Press.

Berry, Brian J. 1980. "Urbanization and Counterurbanization in the United States." *Annals of the American Academy of Political and Social Science* 451: 13–20.

BGS Staff. 2020. "LISTEN: Will Kimbrough, 'My Right Wing Friend.'" *The Bluegrass Situation,* September 10, 2020.

Blayney, George Cadwallader. 1850. "Stereotyping." *Scientific American* 6 (14): 108.

Bleiberg, Jake, and Seth Koenig. 2017. "'Donald Trump with a Maine Accent' Sentenced to Four Months for Illegal Campaign Donations." *Bangor Daily News,* August 9, 2017.

Boatright-Horowitz, Su L., Marissa E. Marraccini, and Yvette Harps-Logan. 2012. "Teaching Antiracism: College Students' Emotional and Cognitive Reactions to Learning about White Privilege." *Journal of Black Studies* 43 (8): 893–911.

Bonilla-Silva, Eduardo. 2003. *Racism without Racists: The Persistence of Racial Inequality in America.* Lanham, Md.: Rowman and Littlefield.

Bonilla-Silva, Eduardo, and David Dietrich. 2011. "The Sweet Enchantment of Color-Blind Racism in Obamerica." *Annals of the Academy of Political and Social Science* 634 (1): 190–206.

Bonnette, Lakeyta. 2015. *Pulse of the People: Political Rap Music and Black Politics.* Philadelphia: Univ. of Pennsylvania Press.

Brewer, Marilynn B. 1979. "In-Group Bias in the Minimally Inter-Group Situation: A Cognitive Motivational Analysis." *Psychology Bulletin* 86: 307–324.

Chiricos, Ted, Kelly Welch, and Marc Gertz. 2004. "Racial Typification of Crime and Support for Punitive Measures." *Criminology* 42: 358–390.

Cooper, Leonie. 2020. "Charley Crockett: 'I don't look like what a country audience expects.'" *The Guardian,* July 10, 2020.

Couto, Richard A., and Catherine S. Guthrie. 1999. *Making Democracy Work Better: Mediating Structures, Social Capital, and the Democratic Prospect.* Chapel Hill: Univ. of North Carolina Press.

Darden, Robert. 2004. *People Get Ready! A New History of Black Gospel Music.* New York: Continuum International Publishing.

Dawidoff, Nicholas. 1997. *In the Country of Country: A Journey to the Roots of American Music.* New York: Vintage Books/Random House.

Delli Carpini, Michael X., and Scott Keeter. 1991. "Stability and Change in the U.S. Public's Knowledge of Politics." *Public Opinion Quarterly* 55: 583–612.

Du Bois, W. E. B. 1903. *The Souls of Black Folks.* Chicago: A. C. McClurg.

Dunaway, David King, and Molly Beer. 2010. *Singing Out: An Oral History of America's Folk Music Revivals.* New York: Oxford Univ. Press.

Dunlap, James. 2006. "Through the Eyes of Tom Joad: Patterns of American Idealism, Bob Dylan and the Folk Protest Movement." *Popular Music and Society* 29: 549–573.

Durcholz, Daniel. 2018. "Singer-Songwriter Ray Wylie Hubbard Confronts His Own Mortality on New Album." *St. Louis Post-Dispatch,* June 1, 2018, www.stltoday.com/entertainment/music/singer-songwriter-ray-wylie-hubbard-confronts-his-mortality-on-new-album/article_a75a157a-d2d2-5d76-a770-2e5559f5978f.html.

Easton, David. 1965. *A Framework for Political Analysis.* Englewood Cliffs, N.J.: Prentice-Hall.

Folk Alliance International. 2021. "About Folk Alliance International." https://folk.org/about/.

Fitzgerald, Kaitlin, and Melanie C. Green. 2017. "Narrative Persuasion: Effects of Transporting Stories on Attitudes, Beliefs, and Behaviors." In *Narrative Absorp-*

tion, edited by Frank Hakemulder, Moniek M. Kuijpers, Ed. S. Tan, Kaitlin Balint, and Murina M. Doicaru, 49–67. Amsterdam/Philadelphia: John Benjamins Publishing Company.

Flynn, D. J., Brendan Nyhan, and Jason Reifler. 2017. "The Nature and Origins of Misperceptions: Understanding False and Unsupported Beliefs about Politics." *Political Psychology* 38: 127–150.

Fording, Richard C., Joe Soss, and Sanford F. Schram. 2011. "Race and the Local Politics of Punishment in the New World of Welfare." *American Journal of Sociology* 116: 1610–1657.

Fontenot, Kayla, Jessica Semega, and Melissa Kollar. 2018. "Income and Poverty in the United States: 2017." *U.S. Census Bureau.* Report number P60-263. Washington, D.C.: GPO.

Fraser, Max. 2018. "Down in a Hole: Outlaw Country and Outlaw Culture." *Southern Cultures* 24 (3): 83–100.

Freeman, Jon. 2021. "Aaron Lee Tasjan Explores Self-Doubt and Sexuality on Biographical New Album." *Rolling Stone,* February 9, 2021.

Gage, Jeff. 2018. "See Jason Isbell's Brooding 'White Man's World' From '2018 AmericanaFest': Intense Performance Is a Highlight of the Americana Honors and Awards, Which Air on CMT on December 6." *Rolling Stone,* December 3, 2018.

Gibson, James L. 1992. "Alternative Measures of Political Tolerance: Must Tolerance Be 'Least-Liked'?" *American Journal of Political Science* 36: 560–577.

Gierzynksi, Anthony. 2018. *The Political Effects of Entertainment Media: How Fictional Worlds Affect Real World Political Perspectives.* Lanham, Md.: Lexington Books.

Gierzynski, Anthony, with Kathryn Eddy. 2013. *Harry Potter and the Millenials: Research Methods and the Politics of the Muggle Generation.* Baltimore: Johns Hopkins Univ. Press.

Gilens, Martin. 1996. "'Race-Coding' and White Opposition to Welfare." *American Political Science Review* 90 (3): 593–604.

——. 1999. *Why Americans Hate Welfare: Race, Media, and the Politics of Antipoverty Policy.* Chicago: Univ. of Chicago Press.

Gilliam, Franklin D., and Shanto Iyengar. 2000. "Prime Suspects: The Influence of Local Television News on the Viewing Public." *American Journal of Political Science* 44: 560–573.

Goldberg, David T. 1994. "Introduction: Multicultural Conditions." In *Multiculturalism: A Critical Reader,* edited by David T. Goldberg. Cambridge, Mass.: Blackwell.

Grant, Marshall. 2006. *I Was There When It Happened: My Life with Johnny Cash.* Nashville, Tenn.: Cumberland House.

Green, Melanie C., and Timothy C. Brock. 2000. "The Role of Transportation in the

Persuasiveness of Public Narratives." *Journal of Personality and Social Psychology* 79: 701–721,

Grimshaw, Michael. 2002. "'Redneck Religion and Shitkickin' Saviors?': Gram Parsons, Theology, and Country." *Popular Music* 21 (1): 93–105.

Gubitz, S. R., and Denzel Avant. 2020. "Racializing Captain America: How Racial Attitudes Affect Perceptions of Affirmative Action and Diversity Initiatives in Media." *Journalism and Mass Communication Quarterly* 97 (3): 683–703.

Hayes, Danny, and Jennifer L. Lawless. 2015. "As Local News Goes, So Goes Citizen Engagement: Media, Knowledge, and Participation in US House Elections." *Journal of Politics* 77: 447–462.

Henry, P. J., and David O. Sears. 2002. "The Symbolic Racism 2000 Scale." *Political Psychology* 23: 253–283.

Hermes, Will. 2013. "Album Reviews: Southeastern." *Rolling Stone,* June 17, 2013.

Hetherington, Marc, and Jonathon Weiler. 2018. *Pickup or Prius: How the Answers to Four Simple Questions Explain America's Great Divide.* Boston, Mass.: Houghton Mifflin Harcourt.

Hertzke, Allen D., Laura K. Olson, Kevin R. den Dulk, and Robert Booth Fowler. 2018. *Religion and Politics in America: Faith, Culture, and Strategic Choices.* New York: Routledge.

Hight, Jewly. 2021. "Amythyst Kiah Found Her Powerful Voice. Now She Has a Sound to Match It." *New York Times,* June 14, 2021.

Hill, Evan, Ainara Tiefenthaler, Christiaan Triebert, Drew Jordan, Haley Willis, and Robin Stein. 2020. "How George Floyd Was Killed in Police Custody." *New York Times,* May 31, 2020.

Hinkle, Steve, and Rupert Brown. 1990. "Intergroup Comparisons and Social Identity: Some Links and Lacune." In *Social Identity Theory: Social and Critical Advances,* edited by D. Abrams and M. A. Hogg, 48–70. New York: Springer-Verlag.

Hofstede, Geert. 2001. *Culture's Consequences: Comparing Values, Behaviors, Institutions, and Organizations across Nations,* 2nd ed. Thousand Oaks, Calif.: Sage.

Holbrook, R. Andrew, and Timothy G. Hill. 2006. "Agenda-Setting and Priming in Prime Time Television: Crime Dramas as Political Cues." *Political Communication* 22 (3): 277–295.

Honky Tonk Amnesia. 1984. KCSN, Northridge, California.

Huddy, Leonnie, Lilliana Mason, and Lene Aaroe. 2015. "Expressive Partisanship: Campaign Involvement, Political Emotion, and Partisan Identity." *American Political Science Review* 109: 1–17.

Hurwitz, Jon, and Mark Peffley. 2005. "Playing the Race Card in the Post–Willie Horton Era: The Impact of Racialized Code Words on Support for Punitive Crime Politics." *Public Opinion Quarterly* 69 (1): 99–112.

Inglehart, Ronald. 1997. *Modernization and Postmodernization: Cultural, Economic, and Political Change in 43 Societies.* Princeton, N.J.: Princeton Univ. Press.

Jackson, Jerma A. 2004. *Singing in My Soul: Black Gospel Music in a Secular Age.* Chapel Hill: Univ. of North Carolina Press.

Jamieson, Kathleen Hall. 1992. *Dirty Politics: Deception, Distraction, and Democracy.* New York: Oxford Univ. Press.

Kallen, Stuart A. 1955. *The Music Library: The History of Country Music.* Farmington Hill, Mich.: Cengage.

Kellstedt, Lyman A. 1989. "The Meaning and Measurement of Evangelicalism: Problems and Prospects." In *Religion and Political Behavior in the United States,* edited by Ted. G. Jelen, 3–22. New York: Praeger.

Kinder, Donald R., and Lynn M. Sanders. 1981. *Divided by Color: Racial Politics and Democratic Ideals.* Chicago: Univ. of Chicago Press.

Kluckhohn, Cylde. 1951. "Values and Value Orientation in the Theory of Action." In *Toward a General Theory of Action,* edited by T. Parsons and E. A. Shils. Cambridge, Mass.: Harvard Univ. Press.

Knapp, Gwendolyn. 2012. "Waiting for Ste. Anne: Herein Lies the True Spirit of Carnival." MyNewOrleans.com, February 1, 2012.

Lippmann, Walter. 1922. *Public Opinion.* New York: Macmillan.

Lomax, Alan, and John Lomax. 1934. *American Ballads and Folk Songs.* New York: Macmillan.

Lomax, Alan, John Lomax, and Ruth Crawford Seeger. 1941. *Our Singing Country: Folk Songs and Ballads.* New York: Macmillan.

Lornell, Kip. 2012. *Exploring American Folk Music: Ethnic, Grassroots, and Regional Traditions in the United States,* 3rd ed. Jackson: Univ. Press of Mississippi.

Malone, Bill C. 2002. *Don't Get Above Your Raisin': Country Music and the Southern Working Class.* Urbana: Univ. of Illinois Press.

Mason, Lilliana, and Julie Wronski. 2018. "One Tribe to Bind Them All: How Our Social Group Attachments Strengthen Partisanship." *Political Psychology* 39: 257–277.

McCarthy, Angela Farizo, Laura K. Olson, and James C. Garrand. 2019. "Religious Right, Religious Left, Both or Neither? Understanding Religio-Political Identifications." *Journal for the Scientific Study of Religion* 58: 547–569.

McConahay, John B. 1986. "Modern Racism, Ambivalence, and the Modern Racism Scale." In *Prejudice, Discrimination, Racism: Theory and Research,* edited by J. F. Dovidio and S. L. Gaertner. New York: Academic Press.

Mier, Tomas. 2021. "Brandi Carlile Says She's 'Disappointed' at Grammys for Changing Song Category from Americana to Pop." *People.com,* October 27, 2021.

Moreau, Julie, Stephen Nuno-Perez, and Lisa M. Sanchez. 2019. "Intersectionality, Linked-Fate, and LGBTQ Participation." *Political Research Quarterly* 72: 976–990.

Morris, R. W. 1983. *Buford: The True Story of "Walking Tall" Sheriff Buford Pusser.* Shiloh, Tex.: Poplar Books.

Moss, Marissa. 2017. "Hear Jason Isbell Confront Privilege in 'White Man's World': Singer-Songwriter Examines Racial Inequality in Latest from 'The Nashville Sound.'" *Rolling Stone,* June 1, 2017.

Mutz, Diana C. 2016. "Harry Potter and the Deathly Donald." *PS: Political Science and Politics* 49: 722–729.

Obama, Barack, and Bruce Springsteen. 2021. *Renegades: Born in the USA.* New York: Crown (Penguin Random House).

Peffley, Mark, and Jon Hurwitz. 2002. "The Racial Components of 'Race-Neutral' Crime Policy Attitudes." *Political Psychology* 23 (1): 59–75.

——. 2010. *Justice in America: The Separate Realities of Blacks and Whites.* Cambridge: Cambridge Univ. Press.

Peffley, Mark, Jon Hurwitz, and Paul Sniderman. 1997. "Racial Stereotypes and Whites' Political View of Blacks in the Context of Welfare and Crime." *American Journal of Political Science* 41 (1): 30–60.

Pettigrew, Thomas F., and Roel W. Meertens. 1995. "Subtle and Blatant Prejudice in Western Europe." *European Journal of Social Psychology* 25: 57–75.

Pew Research Center. 2015. "America's Changing Religious Landscape: Christians Decline Sharply as Share of the Population; Unaffiliated and Other Faiths Continue to Grow." *Pew Research Center,* May 12, 2015.

Putnam, Robert. 2000. *Bowling Alone: The Collapse and Revival of the American Community.* New York: Simon and Schuster.

Rector, Lucy Holman. 2008. "Comparison of Wikipedia and other encyclopedia for accuracy, breadth, and depth in historical articles." *Reference Services Review.* 36 (1): 7–22.

Roy, William G. 2010. *Reds, Whites and Blues: Social Movements, Folk Music, and Race in the United States.* Princeton, N.J.: Princeton Univ. Press.

Saviano, Tamara. 2016. *Without Getting Killed or Caught: The Life and Music of Guy Clark.* College Station, Tex.: Texas A&M Univ. Press.

Schwartz, Ian. 2020. "President Trump Visits St. John's Church, Holds Up Bible." *RealClear Politics,* June 1, 2020.

Sears, David O. 1986. "College Sophomores in the Laboratory: Influences of a Narrow Database on Social Psychology's View of Human Nature." *Journal of Personality and Social Psychology* 51: 515–530.

——. 1988. "Symbolic Racism." In *Eliminating Racism: Profiles in Controversy,* edited by Phyllis A. Katz and Dalmas A. Taylor. New York: Plenum.

Seely, Mike. 2014. "James McMurtry's Continental Riffs." *No Depression,* October 3, 2014.

Seilman, Uffe, and Steen F. Larsen. 1989. "Personal Resonance to Literature: A Study of Remindings while Reading." *Poetics* 18: 165–177.

Shanahan, Sue. 2017. "Rodney Crowell: It Ain't Over Yet." *Huffpost,* March 29, 2017.

Sirin, Cigdem V., Nicholas A. Valentino, and José D. Villalobos. 2017. "The Social Causes and Political Consequences of Group Empathy." *Political Psychology* 38: 427–448.

——. 2021. *Seeing Us in Them: Social Divisions and the Politics of Group Empathy.* New York: Cambridge Univ. Press.

Sirin, Cigdem V., José D. Villalobos, and Nicholas A. Valentino. 2016. "Group Empathy Theory: The Effect of Group Empathy on US Intergroup Attitudes and Behavior in the Context of Immigration Threats." *Journal of Politics* 78: 893–908.

Smith, Laura. 2017. "The Man Responsible for the Modern NRA Killed a Hispanic Teenager before Becoming a Border Agent." *Timeline,* www.timeline.com/harlon-carter-nra-murder-2f8227f2434f.

Spence, Lester K. 2011. *Stare in the Darkness: The Limits of Hip-Hop and Black Politics.* Minneapolis: Univ. of Minnesota Press.

Streissguth, Michael. 2013. *Outlaw: Willie, Waylon, Kris, and the Renegades of Nashville.* New York: HarperCollins.

Stouffer, Samuel A. 1955. *Communism, Conformity, and Civil Liberties.* Garden City, N.J.: Doubleday.

Sullivan, James. 2013. "Jason Isbell: 'There's Still Just as Much Awe' in Sobriety: Former Drive-By Trucker Is Enjoying a Breakout Moment with New Album 'Southeastern.'" *Rolling Stone,* August 1, 2013.

Sullivan, John L., James Piereson, and Marcus E. George. 1979. "A Reconceptualization of Political Tolerance: Illusory Increases, 1950s–1970s." *American Political Science Review* 75: 92–106.

——. 1982. *Political Tolerance and American Democracy.* Chicago, Ill.: Univ. of Chicago Press.

Tajfel, Henri, and John Turner. 1979. "An Integrated Theory of Intergroup Conflict." In *The Social Psychology of Intergroup Relations,* edited by W. G. Austin and S. Worchel, 33–47. Monterey, Calif.: Brooks/Cole.

Tichi, Cecilia. 1994. *High and Lonesome: The American Culture of Country Music.* Chapel Hill: Univ. of North Carolina Press.

"Tim O'Brien and Jan Fabricius 'Sodbuster' WDVX Live From Home." 2021. *YouTube,* May 7, 2021.

Travers, Andrew. 2019. "Son Volt's Jay Farrar Discusses Protest Record 'Union' and Headlining Belly Up Aspen." *Aspen Times,* August 21, 2019.

Valentino, Nicholas. 1999. "Crime News and the Priming of Racial Attitudes during Evaluations of the President." *Public Opinion Quarterly* 63 (3): 293–320.

Vetter, Matthew A. 2018. "Teaching Wikipedia: Appalachian Rhetoric and the Encyclopedic Politics of Representation." *College English.* 80(5): 397–422.

Ward, Brian. 1998. *Just My Soul Responding: Rhythm and Blues, Black Consciousness, and Race Relations.* Berkeley: Univ. of California Press.

Weber, Christopher R., Howard Levine, Leonie Huddy, and Christopher M. Federico. 2014. "Placing Racial Stereotypes in Context: Social Desirability and the Politics of Racial Hostility." *American Journal of Political Science* 58 (1): 63–78.

Whitehead, Andrew L. 2014. "Politics, Religion, Attribution Theory, and Attitudes toward Same-Sex Unions." *Social Science Quarterly* 95: 701–718.

Zimmerman, Lee David. 2020. *Americana Music: Voices, Visionaries and Pioneers of an Honest Sound.* College Station, Tex.: Texas A&M Univ. Press.

INDEX